THE TRAVELLERS' LIBRARY

★

TWENTY-FIVE

¶ A descriptive list of some of the volumes in THE TRAVELLERS' LIBRARY can be obtained from any bookseller, or from the publishers.

25

BEING A YOUNG MAN'S CANDID RECOLLECTIONS
OF HIS ELDERS AND BETTERS

by

BEVERLEY NICHOLS

LONDON
JONATHAN CAPE 30 BEDFORD SQUARE

FIRST PUBLISHED 1926
FIRST ISSUED IN THE TRAVELLERS' LIBRARY 1930
REPRINTED 1931
REPRINTED 1931
REPRINTED 1932
REPRINTED 1933
REPRINTED 1934
REPRINTED 1934
REPRINTED 1936
REPRINTED 1941

JONATHAN CAPE LTD. 30 BEDFORD SQUARE LONDON
& 91 WELLINGTON STREET WEST, TORONTO

PRINTED IN GREAT BRITAIN BY
THE GARDEN CITY PRESS LIMITED
LETCHWORTH HERTS & LONDON
AND BOUND BY A. W. BAIN & CO. LTD.
PAPER MADE BY SPALDING & HODGE LTD.
LONDON

CONTENTS

to

GEORGE AND BLANCHE

FOREWORD

Twenty-five seems to me the latest age at which anybody should write an autobiography. It has an air of finality about it, as though one had clambered to the summit of a great hill, and were waving good-bye to some very distant country which can never be revisited.

A delicious age, you may agree, but an age too irresponsible for the production of autobiographies. Why, I ask you? The bones of a young man of twenty-five (according to the medical profession) are duly set, his teeth are ranged in their correct places, and many arid pastures have been made beautiful by the sowing of his wild oats. Why then, not write about some of the exciting people he has seen, while they still excite him?

That is the essence of the whole matter, to write of these things before it is too late. This is an age of boredom, and by the time one is thirty, I am terribly afraid that the first flush of enthusiasm may have worn off. It is quite possible that by then I shall no longer be thrilled by the sight of Arnold Bennett twisting his forelock at a first night, and that the vision of Elinor Glyn eating quantities of cold ham at the Bath Club (a sight which, to-day, never fails to amuse) will not move me in the least.

It is also possible that my indignations will have suffered a similar cooling, that I shall no longer feel faintly sick at the sight of the new Regent Street, and shall be able to view the idolization by the British people of Mr. George Robey, if not with approbation, at least with tolerance.

It is to be hoped that this will not be the case, but

you must admit, from your own experience of young men who have grown up, that it is quite on the cards. They are faithless to their first hates, they have forgotten their first loves. They turn from the dreams of Oxford to the nightmares of the city, just because the dream is difficult, and the nightmare is so easy. In fact, they grow old.

That is why I have written this book. And from the decrepitude of thirty I shall write another on the same lines. It will be called 'Making the Most of Twenty-Eight.'

B. N.

CHAPTER ONE

In which some English Gentlemen set out on a Strange Journey

HAD one been a Prime Minister there would be every reason for talking of one's first tooth and devoting a chapter or two to its effect upon the history of our times. There would then follow, in succeeding volumes, sketches of the youthful genius from every aspect, with appropriate legends at the top of each page, such as 'Backward at School,' 'A Daring Frolic,' 'Visit to the Tomb of William Pitt.'

But since one has not been a Prime Minister, and since all first teeth greatly resemble one another, and since most small boys are very much alike (for if they aren't, they are horrid) — since, in fact, there is no excuse for being dull, we must begin by making things happen. And I can think of no better moment for ringing up the curtain than when, at the age of nineteen, two months before the Armistice, I was given leave to go to America as Secretary to the British Universities Mission to the United States.

It sounds deadly, but it was really exceedingly amusing, for this mission, before it finished its tour (which was largely for propaganda purposes), was to come in touch with most of the leading men in America, from President Wilson downwards. Even in England, there were celebrities hanging round us, all telling us with various degrees of pomposity the sort of things which Americans expected Englishmen to do, and the best way not to do them.

Ian Hay was the first man who gave me any information about America that was worth having. I can see him now, standing against a window in the

Ministry of Information, a tall, slim figure, in a rather shabby uniform, saying:

'Whatever else you do, don't refer to the Americans as "children." It's such a damned insult.'

I demanded further suggestions.

'Dozens, if you want them. Don't leave your boots outside the hotel door. Don't get ruffled if a porter slaps you on the back and calls you "boy." Don't be surprised if they refer to their country as the peculiar property of the Almighty. For all you know they may be right. It's a marvellous country. And the people! Lovable isn't the word for them. They'll kill you with kindness.'

All this I had heard before, but from Ian Hay it sounded different. It is not surprising that he was a success in the States. He is very like his own heroes, who, even when they are talking fourteen to the dozen, give one the impression of being strong and silent. Add to this quality a charming smile, the faintest possible flavour of a Scottish accent, and an air of modesty which is not usually associated with the Creators of best-sellers, and you will have the main ingredients of one of our most typical authors.

If Ian Hay had accompanied us on our Mission he would have had material for a comic masterpiece of English literature. There was the representative of Oxford, who was to lose his boots in every American hotel we were to frequent. There was dear old Sir Henry Jones, whose Scottish-Welsh accents, combined with a heavy beard, an almost complete lack of teeth, and a heavenly smile, were so to intrigue American audiences; Professor J—, the brilliant

Irish scientist, who was our official pessimist, and foretold shipwreck, train-wreck, and motor-wreck with unfailing hope; Sir Henry Miers, from Manchester, cool, calm, and capable, who found the Oxford representative's boots for him and helped to interpret some of Sir Henry Jones's more obscure utterances; and last, but certainly not least, Sir Arthur Shipley, the urbane Vice-Chancellor of Cambridge, who never lost his boots, who spoke perfect English, who had always exactly the right word to say to exactly the right person, and without whom we should all probably have been arrested within twenty-four hours of our arrival as a band of undesirable mountebanks.

I wonder if all the English missions which tour the United States, which march in dignified processions through the streets, which blink up at the skyscrapers, which sneeze over the grape-juice and stagger back from the serried headlines of the newspapers . . . I wonder if they are all made up from such human and fallible men as was ours.

Take the case of Sir Henry Jones, one of the sweetest characters and the most generous men I have ever met. He had, in his head, a tooth. One tooth, and no more. The first memory I have of him was in the early morning, when we were ploughing our way through a choppy sea, with the coast of Scotland misty to the starboard. He put his head through my porthole, and complained bitterly that there was no fresh water in his cabin. 'What did he want fresh water for?' I asked, looking sleepily at his flowing beard. He waved his toothbrush through the window, and I gave him my carafe. I wish we were all such optimists. And I hope this story is not too impertinent. A very faint hope, I fear.

Again, Professor J — . It is with no lack of respect that I refer to the more humorous side of his character. Any scientist, from San Francisco to Petrograd, will tell you what the world of astronomy owes to his researches into the theory of the Martian canals. Anybody but a fool would pay homage to his intellect. None the less, for sheer pessimism I have never met his like.

'I took a bath this morning,' he said to us, one day at breakfast, 'and I did it at the peril of my life.'

We wondered what made him think that a bath was so particularly perilous. He explained. In taking his bath it had been necessary for him to take off his patent waistcoat. It had also been necessary for him to take off his clothes. In view of the fact that we were at the moment, in a part of the ocean which was regarded with particular affection by German submarines, both actions had been highly inadvisable. The patent waistcoat for obvious reasons. The dangers of the state of nature, however, he described at greater length. 'If a body enters the water,' he said, 'death takes place by chill just as often as by actual drowning. I have made researches into the matter and I find that a body covered with clothes does not chill so fast as a body with nothing on. Hence the danger of baths in a situation such as this. Supposing a torpedo had hit us while I was in my bath!'

While we were on the water, a torpedo did actually hit a liner off the Coast of Ireland, though it was not our own vessel. As soon as the news came through, J — was convinced that one of his own relatives, an aged aunt, must have been on board. The fact that she had been bedridden for eight years, the fact that there was no conceivable reason why she should have got up at all, far less have ventured across the Atlantic, weighed with him not at all. He was born like that, and I think he even took a certain grim pleasure in it, realizing the futility of human existence.

When I add that there were in our Mission two ladies, Miss Spurgeon and Miss Sedgwick, the introductory passage to this book is complete.

Have you ever noticed – you who have crossed the Atlantic – the extraordinary effect that the Statue of Liberty has upon those who pass for the first time beneath its shadow? It brings out all sorts of hidden traits in even the most secretive of the passengers. Men who have spent the entire voyage in the bar, whom nobody would accuse of sentimentality, rush out and stand strictly to attention, chin well out, eyes fixed on that impressive brazen lady, much as a dog would fix its eyes on its mistress. Young and flapping ladies, who have lain on the decks in attitudes which they apparently consider seductive, stand with open mouths and unpowdered noses, trying to remember the date of the American Declaration of Independence. Fathers bring out their children and regard the statue with an air of proprietorship as though they themselves had been largely responsible for its erection. And as for the poets . . .

We had on board one rather celebrated young poet who I am sure will never forget the Statue of Liberty – whether or no the statue will ever forget him is another question. His name was Robert Nichols, and he was being sent out by the English Government as the most accomplished of all our war poets. He had created rather a sensation at home by his volume, *Ardours and Endurances*, which contained, in the opinion of the critics, much the best war poetry which had been produced. During the voyage over I fear he had not been much in the mood for writing poetry, unless it were of the style of Rupert Brooke's dreadful 'Channel Crossing,' for he had been groaning with sea-sickness in his cabin. But the statue cured him of all that. As soon as he heard that we were about to pass under it, he emerged pale but determined and came up to me, where I was standing by the railings.

'I'm going to salute the statue,' he said.

'Well, hadn't you better get your hat?' I asked. 'You can't salute without a hat on.'

'I don't care a damn about the hat,' replied Robert, and without any more ado, swung his hand behind his ear, where it remained quivering like any guardsman's. Further conversation under these circumstances would, I realized, be sacrilege not only on the spirit of liberty but on the spirit of poetry as well, and so I held my peace. But it was a pity that Robert had somewhat miscalculated the distance we still had to run, for after a few minutes he was forced, from sheer cramp, to lower his arm again. It would have been better if he had got his hat.

I fear that Robert Nichols did not greatly enjoy himself in the States. He could not get that 'platform' which had been anticipated for him, and he always looked a little afraid, when one saw him on

Fifth Avenue, as though a skyscraper would fall on him before he had finished his last sonnet. He might indeed have been reading a Keats poem:

> When I have fears that I may cease to be
> Before my pen has gleamed my teeming brain,
> Before high-piled books, in charact'ry
> Hold like full garners the full-ripen'd grain . . .

All of this, however, is not getting us to America, to Presidents and millionaires, and all those other engaging things.

Landing in America in this autumn of 1918, for an Englishman at least, was exactly like a page out of an H. G. Wells novel. The aeroplanes circling round us, the little pilot boat coming with newspapers that told us the end of the war was in sight, the sudden glimpse of a new radiant continent, with houses sparkling with a million lights – it was the lights that we found most surprising. After stumbling about in darkened streets at home, after being given hell by the police if we so much as allowed a chink of light to escape through the window (for fear of air raids, of course), it seemed almost indecent to see this blaze of light coming from every window. In absolute exultation, as soon as I reached my room (we were staying at the Columbia University Club), I turned on all the lights, drew the curtain, and threw open the window, thinking – 'there, look at that, and be damned to you,' the remark being addressed to imaginary zeppelins, thousands of miles away.

And then – the banquet that night! There was butter. Lots of it, making the pale wisps of grease on which we had lately fed seem like some loathsome memory of a nightmare. There was sugar, not done up in little bags, and shrunk to the size of a pea, but fat, glistening sugar, shining and sparkling like any diamond. There was meat, not brought to one in exchange for a coupon, but perched on the plate, proud and abundant. Sir Henry Jones's one tooth was working overtime that night.

At this dinner I met my First Great American – Nicholas Murray Butler – President of Columbia University.

For the benefit of English readers I should here point out that the Presidents of great American Universities occupy far more prominent positions in the life of the nation than the Vice-Chancellors of Oxford or Cambridge. These latter gentlemen are hardly known to the public at all. The only Vice-Chancellor of Oxford of whom the newspaper-reading public has ever heard is Ex-Vice-Chancellor Farnell, who set the whole University on edge by medieval restrictions, and who has now retired to the obscurity from which his faintly ridiculous personality should never have been dragged. Apart from this regrettable exception, English Vice-Chancellors have usually figured only in small paragraphs at the bottom of the sober columns of *The Times*, when they are reported as having given degrees to various earnest youths and maidens.

In America it is very different. Here, when the President of a great college delivers himself of an utterance, great treble headings announce the fact in all the principal newspapers. He is given almost as much publicity as a successful horse. His judgments are made the subject of leading articles, his portrait is almost as well known as that of the baser type of politician in England. I do not know whether this is because knowledge is more venerated in the United States than in England. It just happens to be the case.

Well, Nicholas Murray Butler was a super-President, and, next to President Wilson and Charlie Chaplin, he was the most 'talked-of' man in the States. As I said before, he was the First Great American I met, and it is with a feeling of regret that I have to admit that I was not in the least impressed. He struck me as the epitome of the commonplace. Charming, yes – a dear, kind smile, a loud and penetrating voice, but – my God! what a mind! It was stocked with every platitude that has bored us since Adam first yawned into the disillusioned face of Eve.

He made a speech. Such a speech. It was filled with tremendous pauses, in which the hand would be raised, and the finger held aloft, and then, like the booming of a gun, the platitude. For example. Silence. A row of expectant faces, and eager eyes. A row of set mouths (except of those who were munching salted almonds). And then . . . 'I say to you, and I say it as my considered opinion, that War is a terrible thing. It is a cruel thing, ladies and gentlemen, a brutal thing. But . . .' again the silence, and the munching mouths are stilled . . . 'wars happen. They occur. They break out. They are declared. They exist. They . . .'

Oh dear, I thought. If all American speeches are like this, I am in for a bad time. Of course, we were very soon to discover that they weren't, and that

American oratory is among the finest in the world. But Nicholas Murray Butler was a bad beginning. It is a matter of absolute mystery to me how people listen to such things, or how they read his books. For example, I picked up, the other day, a book by him called *Is America Worth Saving?* It was incredible. It contained page after page of the dullest moralization, page after page devoted to the proving that black is generally black, and that white, more often than not, is white. And yet, when you get him by himself, Butler is better. When we went to see him at Columbia University he kept Sir Arthur Shipley and myself giggling faintly for twenty minutes over his description of some of the difficulties of the educational career. I remember in particular one reply he made which was typical of a certain broad, dry humour. Sir Arthur had asked him, with reference to a little party of English boys who had gone out west, if they were still at San Francisco. 'Not always so very still,' replied Butler with a smile.

I had a long talk with Nicholas Murray Butler, but I gained no enlightenment from it. He told me that the young had a great advantage over the old because the young had longer to live, but after all the old had an advantage over the young because they had lived longer. Or some equally penetrating generalization. After talking to him for ten minutes, in an atmosphere of linked Star Spangled Banners and Union Jacks, I came to the conclusion that he probably had so original and destructive a mind that he was forced to send out this smoke-barrage of commonplace in order not to be arrested as a revolutionary.

CHAPTER TWO

Presients – Lean and Fat

I F you wish to sip the very essence of democracy, you must pay a visit to the White House and talk with the President of the United States. The more urgent your business, the more stirring the occasion, the more completely unpretentious will be your reception.

We arrived in Washington in late October, already somewhat battered by an existence in which every meal was a banquet, and on the day after our arrival found ourselves drawing up at the gates of the White House, duly attired, cleaned and brushed, in order to make the most favourable impression on President Wilson.

The simplicity of the first home of America is, in some ways, more alarming than the pomp of an ordinary Court. There were no beautiful footmen, no drifting diplomats to waft us higher and higher until we were at length admitted into the presence. Indeed, it was more like going to see a dentist than a President.

We were shown into a pleasant white room, with the usual dentist's array of newspapers and periodicals, slightly soiled by many democratic thumbs. At this point it might be mentioned that the pet mascot of the Mission also entered the White House with us, concealed in an overcoat. This was Cuthbert, a stuffed rabbit, which had been presented by a frivolous friend to the Mission on our departure from England. Cuthbert had been a sure help in trouble and had grown more than human. When the sea was rough, he would be propped up on the edge, looking over, in case he might be overcome. When it was calm he would be allowed to bask in the sunshine. And when we were passing under the Statue of Liberty he was stood to attention until the statue was passed. He couldn't salute, because toy rabbits aren't made that way.

Cuthbert was adored by every member of the Mission, except the representative of Oxford, who thought that such things were naughty. He was taken to the tops of skyscrapers to survey New York by night. He was taken on the Hudson to survey New York by day. And I was damned if I was going to allow Cuthbert to depart from America without entering the White House. And so, he was carefully stuffed into the capacious pocket of Sir Arthur's overcoat (unknown, one must in fairness admit, to Sir Arthur). He was not taken, however, to see the President. There are limits.

Mr. Lawson, the Secretary for the Interior, was with us when we entered, but the real thrill of the morning was to come when a manservant poked his head through the door and said, 'Are you men waiting to see the President?' We all bridled slightly at this historic question. 'How divinely American!' we thought. Were we 'men' waiting to see the President? Men. *Men*, if you please. The world's greatest authority on bugs. A man. The world's greatest authority on the canals of Mars. A man. The world's greatest authority on Greek something or other. A man. Men – all men. Except, of course, the women. We said, yes, we were waiting to see him.

'Then you'd best come along with me,' said the manservant.

We came along with him. We came along through a passage, from which outside you could see the short drive, the white buildings of Washington, the bustling life of the city passing by, and we stepped through some folding doors, on to a great space of highly polished floor, in the centre of which, like a waxwork, was standing the world's most important figure – President Wilson.

The first thing that struck me was that he looked very clean. Immaculate. Not that I had expected to find him dirty. But there was something about the stiff white cuffs, the gleaming collar, the sparkling pince-nez, the beautifully pressed trousers, that suggested he had dressed in a disinfected room with the assistance of a highly efficient valet, who had put on his clothes with pincers. Again the dentist feeling. He *was* like a dentist. Or a distinguished surgeon.

In silence we were introduced, and slid over the polished floor until we were grouped round him in a sort of semicircle. I had a ridiculous feeling that we were all going to sing 'Here we come gathering nuts-in-May.' Everything was suddenly so dignified. No question now of being mere 'men.' We were all diplomats, in the centre of the universe.

And then Wilson began to speak, quietly and calmly, weighing his words, telling us exactly what was passing in his mind. I remember being struck by two things – foolish, no doubt. The first was a feeling of strangeness that he should speak with an American accent. One had imagined him as belonging to the world, forgetting that after all, he only belonged to America. The second was that he was just an ordinary man, in a hideously difficult position, applying the ordinary standards of decent conduct to the world situation.

He talked about affairs in France, compared them with that of last year, and drew conclusions. And then he said something extraordinarily interesting:

'My principal difficulty,' he remarked, 'is that we are dealing with people whom we can't trust. I wonder if you can understand how baffling that is, when one is honestly trying to find a way out? If Germany were like any other country, if we could count on certain promises, certain assurances being fulfilled, then we should know where we are. But we can't count (he almost shouted the last words) on that. I write a note. I receive an answer. I write another note. I receive another answer. *I go on writing notes.* And I am left in exactly the same situation as before, because I have learnt, from bitter experience, that the promises contained in that answer will be broken as soon as the first convenient opportunity presents itself.'

All the time he spoke he stood looking straight in front of him, with his hands behind his back. He looked terribly tired. I gathered afterwards that he had scarcely time to sleep, that often he would be up all night trying to unravel the hopeless tangle of lies and evasions which was almost daily served up for him.

He continued in this strain for some time, until there suddenly came into his voice a note of passion, 'America is not going to leave the Hohenzollerns in power. It would mean leaving a running sore in the

24

heart of Europe.' He made a little grimace of disgust.

I won't attempt to give any long précis of his remarks. Generalizations are never interesting, and even if they were, you can discover all of them in the newspapers of the period. Sir Arthur had a talk with him on the way out about his life at Princeton, and with his usual genius, managed to smooth the wrinkles out of his face and to make him laugh. The last words I heard him say were in reference to the Princeton professors. 'They kicked me upstairs,' he said. A very long way upstairs, most people would think.

That was one of the most interesting mornings of my life. I only wish that Cuthbert could have been concealed behind the curtain.

Where Wilson impressed one with a feeling of respect (if not reverence), Taft filled one with a bouncing spirit of good will – a sort of 'Pippa Passes' spirit – that as long as Taft was in being, all must be right with the United States.

I met him at a dinner given about this time in Washington, and was at once captivated by him, because he seemed to make a point of being particularly charming to the people who didn't matter. There was a tremendous reception after dinner, and half the time Taft was standing, a round Colossus, talking to persons of no importance, and ignoring the crowd of millionaires and diplomats who clustered round him.

Somehow or other, I found myself talking to him. He said:

'Well, young man, and aren't you getting rather sick of trotting round with a lot of old professors?'

I indignantly disclaimed any such suggestion (which happened to be quite untrue.)

However, Taft only winked, and said Englishmen were always so tactful, weren't they, winked again, heaved his shoulders, and shook. Then, apropos of nothing he said:

'I heard a wonderful story yesterday about a Scotchman.'

One has always just heard wonderful stories about Scotchmen, but not always from Ex-Presidents of the United States, so I listened politely.

'A Scotchman,' said Taft, speaking in a loud whisper, and keeping one eye on the crowd of millionaires behind him, 'went out one cold day on the links, did the whole eighteen holes, tramped back, and at the end of it all gave his caddy three-pence.'

Here he heaved again. I wondered if that was the end of the story, when Taft continued:

'The caddy looked at the man and said, "D'ye ken I can tell yer fortune by these three pennies?" '

(Heavens! I thought. He can speak Scotch. No wonder they made him President of the United States.)

'The man shook his head,' said Taft, 'and the caddy looked at the first penny.

' "The fir-r-rst penny," he said, "tells me that you're a Scotsman. Eh?"

' "Yes."

' "The second tells me that you're a bachelor."

' "Yes."

26

' "And the thir-rd penny tells me that yer father-r was a bachelor too." '

And with that Taft turned on his heel, roaring with laughter, leaving at least one young Englishman a staunch Anglo-American for the rest of his life.

It was also in Washington that I first met Elihu Root. Everybody, ever since my arrival had said, 'Ah! but you must meet Elihu Root,' rather in the same sort of way as Sydney people say, 'Ah! but you must see our harbour,' or Cambridge people, 'Ah! but you must see our Backs.' He seemed to have a quite unique reputation – the reputation of being a thoroughly honest politician. I used to ask, 'Why in that case is he not made President?' And the reply invariably was, 'He is too good, too honest, too impeccable.' All of which seemed very strange.

However, when one met him, the mystery was explained. Elihu Root struck me as 'a very parfit gentle knight.' His conversation was like a man thinking aloud. He shut his eyes and frowned and then spoke, and you knew that the man was telling you what he really thought. It was at one of the inevitable banquets that he first appeared, and after it was over I boldly went up to him and asked him some sort of question about Anglo-American friendship.

'That rests with you, young man,' he said, and shut his eyes. 'Youth to youth, young heart to young heart' – and he sighed a little sentimentally.

I asked him the usual stock question which one asks on these occasions – if there was no means of dissipating some of the ridiculous clouds of mistrust and delusion which still hung over the Atlantic, blotting out the true features of each nation from one another; if there was no means of bringing the Press, at least, to realize the importance of the Anglo-American ideal.

'Ah – the Press. Did you ever study the question of sovereignty at college?' he said.

'Yes.'

'Have you ever tried to put your finger on a certain monarch, a certain body of men, a certain institute and say, "Here is sovereignty – here is the ultimate authority"? And have you, when you have decided that sovereignty lies here, or there, suddenly realized that the true power still eludes you? Have you realized that those men are elected by the people and that in consequence sovereignty lies in the people? And have you, going even further, realized that the force that makes the people vote, i.e. the force that moulds the people's wills, is really the true sovereign? Think about it. And then you will realize the true importance of the remark you made to me just now.'

All this was delivered with eyes shut and with head tilted back. A very straight and honest man, Mr. Root, typical of all that is best in American life.

From Washington we travelled to Boston, staying with President Lowell of Harvard. Harvard made us all feel a little depressed. It was so very rich, so very efficient, so very prosperous, so entirely different from the bankrupt universities of England. I looked with green eyes on undergraduates' rooms fitted with telephones and bathrooms, and served with a

28

central heating apparatus that made the frozen apartments of Balliol seem a little torturous.

And then, after Boston, Chicago. Our arrival in Chicago was sensational. Mr. Hearst, the newspaper proprietor, had declared the war to be over, although it was still raging gaily, and had another forty-eight hours to run. As a result of Mr. Hearst's enterprise, all the country people within a hundred miles of Chicago had come to 'celebrate,' and they travelled with us, dressed in their best, and taking liberal swigs of whisky. When we actually arrived, we found a mad city. Paper littered the streets, bells clanged everywhere. And when we came to the club (decency forbids me to mention which one it was) every waiter in the place was drunk, and we had to tread our way upstairs over recumbent figures, while our bags remained in the hall.

'Terrible,' said the representative of Oxford. 'I am beginning to understand why the Americans have so urgent a need for Prohibition.'

I am afraid I did not agree with him. It all seemed to me very jolly. For one thing, all the telephone books in the club had been taken to the roof where they had, throughout the day, been slowly torn into little pieces by intoxicated fingers, in order that the streets might have a festive and confetti-like appearance. As a result, though we could be rung up, we could not ring up, and that, for the secretary of an educational mission was, I assure you, a blessing not at all in disguise.

However, that was one of the only two occasions when I ever saw anybody intoxicated in America.

The other was some weeks later when we were down in Texas. We had been travelling all night, and we emerged, one cold morning before breakfast, at the town of — (I had better leave it blank), to visit the local university. Half the professorial staff were lined up on the platform to meet us, and they certainly had the warmest ideas of hospitality, for from the overcoat pockets of at least half a dozen of the more venerable members of the staff protruded the neck of a bottle of rye whisky. Now rye whisky is, at all times, a potent drink, but taken before breakfast, on a cold morning, it is not only potent, it is deadly. Nor was this all. For when we had driven to the university, we were greeted by a festive board at which the chief item of diet appeared to be egg-nog, well flavoured with rum. However, we all enjoyed ourselves very much, though I fear that this part of the tour cannot have been very fruitful from the educational point of view, however much it may have strengthened the Anglo-American ties of friendship.

CHAPTER THREE

Containing a Fruitless Search for American Vulgarity

I NOTICED more and more in America that vulgarity (which one finds, of course, all over the world, even in the South Sea Islands), seemed to be in inverse ratio to wealth. The people who were really tiresome, who talked about their automobiles and their incomes, and their emeralds, and their trips to Europe, were nearly always the people with comparatively small incomes. They might be rich, but they weren't 'rolling,' like the Goulds or the Vanderbilts.

For example, a perfectly appalling little woman to whose box at the opera I was once unwillingly lured, suddenly, during an *entr'acte*, produced from her stocking a cheque for a hundred thousand dollars, and waved it in my face, saying, 'Say, what d'you think of that for a birthday present?' A most unsavoury proceeding, and as I afterwards discovered, a complete fake. The woman's husband had not a hundred thousand dollars in the world, and went bankrupt only a few weeks later.

How entirely different are the super-millionaires! They have enough money to roof their houses in gold and diamonds, but they behave with the simplicity of an English parson. It seems foolish to have to say it, and one's only excuse is that there is still in England a ridiculous prejudice against rich Americans.

It would be a good thing if people who have such a prejudice could meet a man like, for example, Jack Pierpont Morgan. No nicer creature ever trod the earth, in spite of his mansions in New York, Grosvenor Square, Scotland, Cannes, and a few other places. He was one of the last people I saw in New York, and one of the best.

One cannot think of Jack Morgan, of course, without thinking of his library, although it is somewhat depressing for an Englishman to think of it, since so vast a multitude of English treasures have found their way there. When he showed me over it I was absolutely staggered by the collection of our manuscripts which is amassed there. There is hardly a novelist or poet of any repute whose faded pages are not treasured in this house. And not only their manuscripts, but their portraits, their personal belongings, in fact anything of interest that is even vaguely connected with them.

I was browsing round among these treasures when I suddenly saw, under a glass case, a thrilling object. It was a little lock of hair, bound together with a piece of ribbon, and underneath was a label which read: 'A lock of the hair of Keats. Given to Shelley by Keats' friend – ' And then there was a description of the time and place at which the lock had been given.

This object so excited me that I could not drag myself away from it.

Jack Morgan came up.

'What are you looking at?' he said. 'Keats' hair? Like to hold it for a minute?'

He produced a key from his pocket, undid the case and put the precious thing into my hand. I felt an almost schoolboy emotion at the thought that this hair had grown from the head in which the Ode to a Grecian Urn had been conceived.

Suddenly Morgan said, 'Give it to me for a moment.'

Reluctantly I handed it over. And then, marvel of marvels, he extracted a single hair from the lock – (a long, curly one) put it on a piece of paper, dropped a spot of sealing wax on one end of it and then wrote, as a sort of testimony:

'Keats' hair. From a lock in my possession. J. P. Morgan.'

This hair he gave to me, and, as all writers of autobiographies so constantly assert, 'it is one of my most treasured possessions.' After he had done that, he took off the key from its ring, handed it to his secretary and said:

'That's the last hair from that lock that I give away. If we take any more we shan't have a lock, we'll have a bald patch. Don't you let me have that key – not if a dozen young Englishmen come along and beg for it on their bended knees.'

Morgan is like a father among his children when he moves among these marvels. He pretends to know nothing very much about them, but he knows a great deal. He knew, for example, what I had never quite understood – the exact sequence in which Poe had written 'The Bells.' Poe's manuscripts seemed to convey a special charm for him, as indeed they might, since Poe was incomparably the greatest creative genius that America has produced. His manuscripts were the very reverse of what one would have expected. There were no wild scrawls, no blotches, no hasty writing. On the contrary, they were all beautifully transcribed on clean paper, in a hand that would have won a prize in the copybook of a schoolboy.

I fell quite in love with American newspapers – bad

taste, I suppose – but quite comprehensible if you have strength enough to survive the first shock of them. Everybody has written everything that there is to be written about American journalism, and I won't add to it. But one episode does deserve to be recorded as a classic example of New World enterprise.

The two ladies of our Mission, after a few weeks of racket and bustle and sleeping-cars, arrived at Detroit in such a state of exhaustion that they retired straight to their rooms, refusing to see anybody, whether they were professors, or journalists, or presidents, no matter, in fact, how distinguished they might be. There arrived on the scene a young man with a speckled face who demanded an immediate interview with these ladies.

'Impossible,' I said.

'I've got to get it.'

'Can't help that.'

'I *shall* get it.'

'You won't.'

Pause. The speckled gentleman spat on the floor, sniffed, and then said, 'Well, we shall see.'

What he meant I did not even guess. But the next day there appeared an immense interview, together with pictures of the two ladies in question, under a head-line that informed all and sundry that 'Dishpans Lose Their Lure For Female Sex in England Say Prominent British Women Educators.'

To an American reader, this must sound quite dull. Its only value, as a story, is that, to an Englishman, it sounds almost impossible. The ladies, rising refreshed, and eating a hearty breakfast, looked up

34

from over their grape-fruit to see this astounding account of the interview which they had never given, and choked with fury.

'How dare they?' said one.

'How monstrous!' said the other. 'Barbarism, savagery!' they cried.

'Not at all.' It was imperative to soothe the ladies a little. 'Don't you see that it's really extraordinarily funny? A speckled young man demands an interview and doesn't get one. He therefore invents it. You ought to feel flattered that your views are so much sought after.'

They did not feel flattered, however.

'Besides,' I added, 'it is probably perfectly true that Dishpans have Lost their Lure. Haven't they?'

'Dishpans have no more to do with the case than the flowers that bloom in the spring,' said the ladies.

And there, I am going to leave America. I am well aware that these few pages represent only a very small and quite superficial fragment of a great many exciting happenings. The truth, however, is that I was too young to pick out what Americans call the 'high spots.' The rest of this book will, I trust, be different.

CHAPTER FOUR

John Masefield, Robert Bridges, W. B. Yeats

IN January, 1919, I went to Oxford. That seems about the shortest way of relating a fact that is of singularly little interest to anybody but myself. What *is* of interest is that Oxford, at that time, was a regular nest of famous singing birds gathered together in the aftermath of the War, choosing Oxford as a sheltered resting-place, as though their wings were a little weary and their feathers rather draggled.

W. B. Yeats had come to rest from the storms of Ireland in a quiet, green-shuttered house in Broad Street; John Masefield was writing his marvellous sonnets in a cottage on Boar's Hill; Robert Bridges, the Poet Laureate, was near by, occasionally producing a few lines of verse which had more satire in them than poetry, to say nothing of such young men as Aldous Huxley, Robert Nichols, and Robert Graves. I must also pay tribute to Leslie Hore-Belisha, who is now perhaps the most brilliant of our younger M.P.'s. He did not write poetry, but his quite unmatched eloquence at the Union will always linger as one of my keenest intellectual (I almost said emotional) pleasures.

Of all these men, by far the greatest, to me at least, was John Masefield. He was the strangest blend of passion, and ethereality. He was, moreover, the most generous of men. As soon as I went to Oxford I decided, in company with a little band of equally impertinent young men, that what Oxford needed was a new literary magazine which should reflect the new spirit of the university after the War. Delicious innocence! One really was under the impression that one was doing something, not only terribly important, but quite new.

After endless cigarettes and a quantity of mulled claret we decided on two things – the title and the price. It was to be called *The Oxford Outlook*, and people were to pay half a crown for it. It is still called *The Oxford Outlook* to this day, which must be something of a record for 'varsity papers. The price, however, is only a shilling.

Now came the question of contributors. Although we were properly idealistic we were also shrewd enough to realize that unless we got some big names, apart from those of the undergraduates, our publication would stand little chance of creating any very great stir in the world outside, which was what we secretly desired. Somebody therefore suggested Masefield. And that night I sat down and wrote to Masefield, telling him what we were doing, and asking him if he could possibly send us a few lines for our first number.

By the next post came a most charming letter from Masefield, wishing us all good luck, and enclosing two of the best sonnets he has ever written – poems which any editor of any country in the world would have been proud to publish. Here is the first of them, which has since been included in the collected edition of his works:

ON GROWING OLD

Be with me, Beauty, for the fire is dying,
  My dog and I are old, too old for roving;
Man, whose young passion sets the spindrift flying
  Is soon too lame to march, too cold for loving.

I take the book and gather to the fire,
  Turning old yellow leaves. Minute by minute
The clock ticks to my heart; a withered wire
  Moves a thin ghost of music in the spinet.

I cannot sail your seas, I cannot wander
  Your mountains, nor your downlands, nor your
    valleys
Ever again, nor share the battle yonder
  Where your young knight the broken squadron
    rallies,
Only stay quiet, while my mind remembers
The beauty of fire from the beauty of embers.

And that he sent to somebody whose name he had
never even heard, knowing full well that we could
not afford to pay for them.

A few weeks later I met Masefield himself. He had
promised to read some of his poetry to a little literary
society which we had gathered together, and we all
assembled in my rooms to await his arrival. It was a
bitterly cold night, with driving snow, and he lived
some eight miles out of Oxford, in a region where
there were neither taxis nor buses, so that he would
have been perfectly justified in 'phoning us to say
that he could not come. However, he turned up
only a few minutes late, having bicycled all the way,
in order not to disappoint us.

One never forgets Masefield's face. It is not the
face of a young man, for it is lined and grave. And
yet it is not the face of an old man, for youth is still
in the bright eyes. Its dominant quality is humility.
There were moments when he seemed almost to
abase himself before his fellow-creatures. And this

humility was echoed in everything he did or said, in the quiet, timid tone of his voice, in the way in which he always shrank from asserting himself.

This quality of his can best be illustrated by his behaviour that night. When the time came for him to read his poems, he would not stand up in any position of pre-eminence but sheltered himself behind the sofa, in the shade of an old lamp, and from there he delivered passages from 'The Everlasting Mercy,' 'Dauber,' 'The Tragedy of Nan,' and 'Pompey the Great.' He talked, too, melodiously, and with the ghost of a question-mark after each of his sentences as though he were saying 'Is this right? Who am I to lay down the law?' And when it was all over, and we began to discuss what he had said, all talking at the top of our voices, very superficially, no doubt, but certainly with a great deal of enthusiasm, it was with a sudden shock that I realized that Masefield had retired into his shell, and was sitting on the floor, almost in the dark, reading a volume of poems by a young and quite unknown writer.

I saw a good deal of him after that. He lived in a little red house looking over the hills and valleys about eight miles out, and on fine days one could see from his window the grey spires and panes of Oxford glittering in the distance.

'Oxford is always different,' he said to me once. 'Always I see her in a new mood of beauty from these hills.' We were looking down on the city from the distance and I too knew how he felt. Oxford from the hills is a dream eternally renewed. Under the rain, when only a few spires and towers rise above the driving sheets of grey, on an April morning, when the whole city is sparkling and dappled with yellow shadows, by moonlight when it is a fantastic vision of the Arabian Nights.

Like many other literary geniuses, Masefield is clever with his hands. He will, with equal complacency, make a model of a ship or mend a garden gate. But since he was himself a sailor — since he has himself known the sea in every mood of loveliness or of terror, it is only natural that, when he does model, he should turn, by instinct, to ships. He showed me, at his house, a most exquisite model in wood of an old sailing vessel of the eighteenth century. There was nothing of the dilettante about that work. Every spar, every rope, every mast, every tiny detail was there, modelled to scale. It would have satisfied the most ardent technician, and yet it had a grace and a poetry that only Masefield could have given it.

'You must keep this in a glass case,' I said to him. 'It's far too precious, too dainty, to knock about like the other things.'

He shook his head. 'She's not going to stay here,' he said. 'I made her for a friend who has been very kind to me.'

That was like Masefield, I thought, to spend weeks and weeks of labour to please 'a friend who had been kind to him.'

Anybody more different from Masefield than the Poet Laureate, Robert Bridges, it would be difficult to imagine. One was always longing to put him on a pedestal, to thrust a sceptre into his hand, and a crown on his head, and then to wait for the lightning. A most leonine and noble gentleman. Even when he wandered round the streets of Oxford clad in shabby knickerbockers, with a large, dirty satchel full of books on his bent back, it was impossible to forget either his great height or the immense head, modelled after Meredith, with a snowy beard and silvery locks, flowing with just that touch of abandon which made one wonder if, after all, Nature had not been a little improved upon.

Just as Masefield's favourite word was Beauty, so, according to popular tradition, Bridges' favourite word was Damn. We all know his celebrated retort to Horatio Bottomley, who had suggested in the House of Commons that in view of the exceedingly limited output of the Poet Laureate, it might be advisable to grant him, instead of his salary, the ancient Poet Laureate's privilege of an annual cask of wine, in order that his tongue might be a little loosened. Bridges, in reply to all these criticisms, merely wrote and said, 'I don't care a damn.' It was typical of him, but most of us thought that the criticism was justified, for, at the time, there *was* a war on, he *was* Poet Laureate, and he *wasn't* writing a word.

The only time I ever heard Bridges deliver himself of this word was at a tea-party at his house on Boar's Hill. He damned the Press, he damned the university, he damned, also, more than one of the modern poets whom we were so ill-advised as to mention. When I mentioned Masefield he was most generous to him, which made me realize how little truth there was in the story which some wit had sent round the university at the time, concerning Bridges' criticism of Masefield. However, though fictitious, it is amusing enough to recall.

' "Masefield's Sonnets"?' he is alleged to have said; 'Ah! yes. Very nice. Pure Shakespeare. Masefield's "Reynard the Fox"? Very nice too. Pure Chaucer. Masefield's "Everlasting Mercy"? Mm. Yes. Pure Masefield.'

The other literary celebrity who at this time had chosen Oxford for a home was the Irish poet, W. B. Yeats. Yeats always seemed to me to move in a mist. He was like 'men as trees walking.' He certainly did not do it on purpose, as Bridges may have done. He would wander along the street with his head in the air and his hands behind his back, always wearing an overcoat, even in the warmest weather, with a long loose bow, and a mouth perpetually open. To walk behind him was in itself an adventure, for when he crossed the street he never took the faintest notice of any traffic that might be bearing down upon him, but dawdled over oblivious of the stream of cars, bicycles, horses and motor-lorries that were rushing past.

A lovable man, Yeats, but, I should imagine, that some people would have found him a trying fellow to live with. When I left my college rooms I went to a divine old house with a rickety staircase, and low ceilings, which looked out on to one of the fairest views in Oxford, the Sheldonian library. To this house after a little time, drifted Yeats, complete with his wife and his baby. It was a time when the servant problem was at its height, and occasionally, if the house was more than usually under-staffed, all the undergraduates and other occupants of rooms, including Yeats himself, used to gather to eat a communal luncheon.

On the first of these luncheons, Yeats arrived very late, and after absently toying for a few moments with a little cold asparagus, turned to me and said:

'Were you at the Union last night?'

'Yes.'

'Well, what did you think of it?'

It was difficult to say what one thought of it. The debate had centred round the ever-green subject of Ireland. There had been a great deal of bad temper, and not very many arguments. Before I could reply Yeats said:

'I thought it was terrible. The appalling ignorance of English Youth about anything remotely connected with Ireland. I was astonished. Why, they don't know the first thing about us.'

He darted a limp stick of asparagus into the open mouth, looked away for a moment and then said:

'Why can't they understand that the Irish people are Irish, and not English? Why can't they realize that over there they've got a race of peasants who believes in fairies, and such-like, and are quite right to do so? Why, I've seen myself the saucers of milk which the Irish peasants have put outside their doors for the pixies to drink.'

He talked absently for a little longer, and then said, in a dreamy voice:

'*If the English could only learn to believe in fairies, there wouldn't ever have been any Irish problem.*'

However, Yeats was not made entirely from dreams. He had a good business streak in him as well. He knew to a 'T' the best market for his poems, although like all poets he also knew from bitter experience that verse as a means of livelihood was impossible.

'America pays best for poetry,' he said to me once; 'but even America pays badly. They will give you twice as much for a poem in America as in England. But for an article they will give you three times as much. I wonder why?'

Among the most entertaining people in Oxford at this time (and, I may add, among the most entertaining people in Europe), were the brothers Sitwell. I suppose the Sitwell trio – Osbert, Sacheverell, and sister Edith, have been talked about as much as any literary family in England. Apart from their merits, they have had a great advantage over most writers to whom publicity is not distasteful – they possess a label. A label is tremendously important if you want to impress yourself on the British public. It seems that there are a certain number of niches in the contemporary temple of Fame, and that unless you fit into one of these niches you will never be recognized. There is a niche labelled 'Paradox Mongers,' another niche labelled 'Psychic Story-tellers' and a whole series of geographical niches labelled 'Dartmoor Scribes,' 'Irish Prophets,' 'Sussex Poets,' 'East End Recorders,' 'Yorkshire Romancers,' etc. If by any chance, a describer of Sussex gorse strayed into the Dartmoor heather, he or she would be disowned. If Mr. Michael Arlen were to get into the wrong omnibus and be observed alighting guiltily at Selfridges, his reputation would be tarnished beyond hope. And if a man who had gained a reputation as a writer of ghost-stories began to make paradoxes, the result, as they say in the Bible, would be confusion.

The particular niche which the Sitwells occupy is that of 'Chelsea de Luxe.' It is a very definite and not unprofitable niche. At the time of which I am writing nobody was inclined to take them seriously. In fact, we used to think that if the Sitwells' papa had been anything else but a baronet with fierce ginger hair, if they themselves had dropped their h's instead of dropping their rhymes, their united efforts would not have created much of a stir, and that *Wheels* (the only true schoolboys' magazine published outside a school) would have been passed over in comparative silence. Since then, however, Osbert has written some of the finest short stories in the English (or the French) language, and Sacheverell has produced a work of real genius in *Southern Baroque Art*.

Sacheverell was 'up' at Oxford at the same time as myself, and introduced a very pleasant flavour of Bohemianism – (there really is no other word) – into those dingy quarters. He hung his rooms with drawings by Picasso and Matisse, which were the subject of lewd comment among the more athletic members of the college. There was one drawing by – I believe, Picasso – called Salome, which represented a skinny and exceedingly revolting old lady prancing in a loathsome attitude before certain generously-paunched old men who looked like the sort of people you meet at a Turkish Bath when your luck is out. One day a certain charming don – (an ardent Roman Catholic) – strolled into Sacheverell's rooms, saw the picture, paled slightly and then asked him what it was all about.

Sacheverell said something about 'line.'

And then the don let go. 'Line,' he said, was the excuse for every rotten piece of work produced by modern artists. If a leg was out of drawing, or a face obviously impossible, if the whole design was grotesque and ridiculous, the excuse was always 'line.' And he stamped out of the room leaving untouched the very excellent lunch which Sacheverell had prepared for him.

But Sacheverell stood his ground in all his conflicts with the authorities. At the end of every term a terrible ordeal takes place known as 'collections,' or more colloquially, 'collecers,' which consists of an examination on the work done during term. When Sacheverell came up for his viva voce, he was greeted with black faces and remarks of that strange and curdled quality which, in academicians, passes for sarcasm. 'As it is obviously superfluous to comment on your knowledge – which is non-existent – we are only left with your style, Mr. Sitwell,' said one of the examiners. 'You appear to write very much in the manner of Ouida.'

'That,' remarked Sacheverell calmly, 'is my aim.'

I am not surprised that Sacheverell describes himself in *Who's Who* as 'Educated Eton College, Balliol College Oxford. Mainly self-educated.'

Osbert, Sacheverell's brother, is the wittiest of God's creatures – (forgive me, Osbert, for that expression) – whom I have ever met. He has infused

46

even more wit than Sacheverell into *Who's Who* —
that badly constructed work of fiction. As far as I
know, the editor of *Who's Who* is not aware of the
pranks which Osbert has played in the 1925 edition.
May I enlighten him?

Take first that wonderful phrase 'Fought in Flan-
ders and farmed with father.' One day I am going
to write a beautiful fugue in F to accompany that
phrase, but at the moment it is only necessary to call
attention to the source from which it sprang. For
that, you must cast your eye to the preceding paragraph, which is devoted to Osbert's papa. There
you will read: 'Being unfit for service, farmed over
2,000 acres, producing great quantities of wheat and
potatoes.'

Take again 'Founded Rememba Bomba League in
1924.' It sounds so exactly like the sort of thing
which most of those who appear in *Who's Who* would
do. There is no such organization as the 'Rem . . .'
No, I won't be quite as obvious as that. But I might
explain that the telegraphic address 'Pauperloo,'
which appears at the bottom of the paragraph'
being interpreted, means 'Pauper Lunatic Asylum.'

'Deeply interested in any manifestation of sport.'
One has a feeling that Osbert's page has got muddled
with that of Lord Lonsdale, or Dame (Clara) Butt.
Until finally, one is informed that his recreations are:
'Regretting the Bourbons, repartee, and Tu Quoque.'

Repartee, most certainly. I have laughed as much
with Osbert as with anybody in the world. I shall
never forget his reply to a certain publisher, who had
been endeavouring, unsuccessfully, to shield the body
of W. J. Turner from the darts of scorn which Osbert

was aiming at it. 'Personally,' said the publisher (and when people begin with that word one always knows they have nothing to say), 'personally, I find W. J. Turner rather a lovable person.'

Osbert put his head on one side and smiled. 'I know what it is,' he said, with an air of discovery, 'you used to keep tadpoles.'

He once told me, with that perfect modesty which his enemies find so disarming, that he gave his superior authorities more trouble during the War than any other officer they had ever known. I suppose it *must* have been a little trying to the colonel who came up to him and asked if he were fond of horses to be told 'No. But I adore giraffes.' And it must have been positively exasperating to the outraged military police to find him, an officer in the Grenadiers, carrying on an intimate conversation with a very private soldier in a very public place. Even worse, when at the subsequent cross-examination, the private soldier turned out to be Epstein (whose taste in birds differs so strangely from that of the British public).

He began a naughty movement during the War to urge that all those who had served in France and had no desire to serve again should first be voluntarily denationalized and then compulsorily deported. It never came to anything. But in spite of its failure, he survived, and still walks from time to time down the grey pavements of Piccadilly, negligently tripping up an occasional poetaster or Royal Academician who has the temerity to cross his path.

One more story. It is set on the said grey pavements, and Osbert was walking over them with

48

another man who was staying with him. There came into sight a mutual acquaintance, whom we will call Lady C. Now Lady C. knew perfectly well that Osbert's friend was staying with him, but she calmly ignored Osbert and said to the friend, 'Do come and dine with me on Friday.' The invitation was accepted. They passed on.

The day of the dinner arrived, and with it, a postcard from Lady C. on Osbert's breakfast table saying, 'I should be so glad if you would come and dine to-night as well as Mr. — '

This was too much. Osbert went grimly to the telephone.

'Hullo? Is that Lady C? I'm sorry, but I shan't be able to dine to-night. But listen. . . . Will you lunch with me last Thursday?'

Yes — England needs its Sitwells.

CHAPTER FIVE

In which Mr. G. K. Chesterton reveals his Fears and his
Hopes

AMONG the questions which will present themselves to the future literary historian, none will
be more difficult to answer than 'Was Mr. G. K.
Chesterton afraid of his wife?' There are several
passages in his books which indicate that the answer
will be in the affirmative, and among them one might
quote that charming essay from *Tremendous Trifles*
which is called 'On Lying in Bed.' He confesses
to an overwhelming desire, while lying in bed, to
paint the ceiling with a long brush. 'But even,' he
adds, 'my proposal to paint on it with the bristly
end of a broom has been discouraged — *never mind
by whom*; by a person debarred from all political
rights.'

The first time I ever asked myself this question was
in Cornmarket Street at Oxford, on a windy night in
May. G. K. Chesterton was alighting, with a certain
amount of difficulty, from a taxi-cab, and as soon as he
had safely emerged, he stood in the gutter, his mackintosh flapping loudly in the wind, while he assisted
a charming and diminutive figure in a cloak. The
diminutive figure was his wife. But even in these
strange circumstances, with the wind tying her cloak
into knots, and the rain-spots slashing against her
veil like cold bullets, she seemed completely mistress
of the situation of the moment, which was 'When
should the car come back to fetch them?'

Chesterton turned to me — (for he had come to
debate with us at the Union) — 'When *shall* we want
it, do you think?' he said, a little pathetically.

Before I could reply the diminutive figure said, in a sweet, firm voice:

'When will the thing be over?' (a great deal of feminine contempt in that sentence).

'At eleven. But there's a sort of reception afterwards.'

She immediately turned to the driver. 'Be here at eleven.'

'But . . .' began Chesterton.

'And,' said Mrs. Chesterton, 'Is this the way in? It's raining, and my husband has a cold.'

So we meekly followed her to the debating hall.

One has so often been told that Chesterton is an enormous, elephantine creature, that the actual sight of him is really a little disappointing. He *is* a big man, of course, but not as big as all that. If it were not for his cloak, and his longish hair, and the bow which he sometimes wears, one would not say that he was an exceptional figure in any way. It seemed to me that he took a secret joy in making himself as large as possible, like some little boy who stuffs his overcoat with cushions. G.K.C. has such a passionate love of the grotesque that if it were suddenly ordained that he should be four times his present size he would give a whoop of joy.

Yes. The more one thinks of it – the more it seems that he *did* purposely accentuate his largeness. His mackintosh was the mackintosh of a man several sizes larger than he. The wide-brimmed Homburg hat seemed specially designed to exaggerate his face. Even his glasses could, without difficulty, have been cut in half. And I noticed that he took a sort of impish delight, as soon as he was introduced to the committee, of placing himself next to the Junior Librarian, a very diminutive young man, whom he addressed as from a pinnacle, holding himself well erect, swelling his shoulders, and even puffing his cheeks, to improve upon the already imposing body with which nature had provided him.

We all trooped into the debating hall, which was absolutely packed, for Chesterton's paradoxes are always a draw with youth. The subject for debate was 'That this house considers that the granting of any further facilities for divorce will be against the true interests of the nation,' or words to that effect. I was speaking against this motion (being one of those who have never seen how the interests of the nation are served by perpetuating the union between a sane husband and a lunatic wife, or a law-abiding wife and a murderer husband), and as soon as my speech was over I went to the 'Ayes' side of the house where Chesterton was sitting and sat beside him.

'You shouldn't have referred to me as eloquent,' he said. 'Wait till you hear me speak. I'm not a bit eloquent. I can't speak off the bat. I must always have notes.'

I looked down and saw that he had a sheet of paper in his hand, on which he had been scribbling in pencil. But the 'notes' were not words, they were little pictures. A grotesque dragon had been hastily drawn in one corner, and a tiny sketch of a very fat man in another. There were also several comic faces, among which I recognized that of the secretary, who was sitting with his profile to us. It was typical of him to call these sketches his 'notes,' and it was even more typical when he got up to make a very brilliant speech, that he left his notes behind him.

I forget what he said except that it struck one as irrelevant. To hear Chesterton speak is in itself an explanation of his writing. He pours out his words, suddenly says something which pleases him by its touch of fantasy, pauses, and then with a face that grows more and more smiling and eyes that grow more and more bright, proceeds to develop the idea, to chase it, to leap ponderously after it, to hurl paradoxes in its wake, to circumvent it with every ingenious conceit. For example, he said, almost in an aside, that doubtless divorce would soon be part of the regular curriculum at Oxford, and when he had said it, was so entranced by the prospect opening up before him, that he almost lost his head, and ended by drawing for us a picture of the future in which M.A. instead of meaning Master of Arts should mean 'married again' and should be accompanied by the B.A., three months later, which would mean 'bachelor again.'

Perhaps his most vivid conversation came after the debate was all over. When we were standing in the hall, waiting for the car, he delivered himself of a second speech which so interested me that afterwards I went straight home to write it down.

'Somebody said in the debate,' he remarked, 'that I am the slave of symbols, that I believed in magic, that in a ceremony or an institution or a faith I merely examined what was on the surface and took it all quite literally, like a peasant in the Middle Ages.

'But it isn't I who am the slave of symbols. It is you. I venerate the idea which lies behind the symbol, you only venerate the empty shell. Take this case of monarchy. Somebody remarked to-night that we had taken away half the duties and prerogatives of the King, and that the monarchy still remained. They went on to say that we could take away half the duties and prerogatives of marriage, and that marriage would still remain. Perhaps it will, but what will be the use of it?

'Because I bow down to the sceptre, and because I take the words "honour and obey" quite literally, you say that I am the slave of the symbol. But I bow down to the sceptre because I believe in the power that lies behind it. I keep to the smallest details of the marriage service because I believe in marriage. If you believe neither in the sceptre nor in the service, and yet bow down to them, then you are the slave of the symbol.'

He looked away. Somebody presented him with his mackintosh. He struggled into it, got it half on, and then, with one arm still waving in the air he exclaimed:

'A time will come – very soon – when you will find that you want this ideal of marriage. You will want it as something hard and solid to cling to in a fast dissolving society. You will want it even more than you seem to want divorce to-day. Divorce . . .' and here, with a sort of groan, he thrust his second arm through his mackintosh – 'the superstition of divorce.'

The small figure of Mrs. Chesterton appeared in the doorway. She, as usual, was quite unperturbed. The fiery words, the tangled eloquence of the evening seemed to have passed over her unnoticed.

'The car is here,' she said, 'and we are already five minutes late.'

G.K.C. shook hands hurriedly, and vanished through the door. The last I saw of him was the flap of his mackintosh in the wind.

CHAPTER SIX

In which Mrs. Asquith behaves with characteristic Energy

OXFORD at this time was a ferment of political activity. It was full of young ex-soldiers, who considered, with pardonable presumption, that having endured Hell for five years, they were justified in suggesting the lines along which the New England (the Lloyd-Georgian England) was to be remodelled. And so we formed ourselves into clubs, concocted newspapers, wore ties varying from the noblest shade of blue to the bloodiest tint of red, and extracted a great deal of pleasure out of it.

On the outskirts of Oxford lived Mr. and Mrs. Asquith, watching with interested eyes this ferment of budding talent. I do not know if Mr. Asquith ever actually said 'Catch 'em young,' but, to use his own type of phraseology, he was not unaware of the advantages which might conceivably be expected from a judicious sowing of the Liberal Seed among mentalities still unprejudiced and alert. It was only to be expected therefore that when I, in company with two staunch friends of the same College, formed the Oxford University Liberal Club, he should accept the position of President with alacrity.

As soon as the club was formed, we arranged a monster meeting in the Oxford Town Hall, and decided that it would be rather fun to have a thoroughly pompous dinner beforehand. We therefore invited various celebrities, who all, to our astonishment, accepted; and when the plans were well in hand, I departed to tell the Master's wife of our intentions.

Now, it has been suggested to me that the Master's wife did not absolutely 'appreciate' Mrs. Asquith. At any rate, although it was understood that Mrs. Asquith was to dine at Balliol, there was trouble. So much trouble, in fact, that it seemed as though the dinner could not take place at all.

This was a dreadful situation. We had already asked Mrs. Asquith to dine. She had already accepted. It was quite impossible to put her off. What was the matter?

It was afterwards suggested to me, by an ingenious scholar of Balliol, that the college authorities feared that Mrs. Asquith would have a disruptive influence on callow youth. A foolish reason, of course. If we wanted, we could have asked Mrs. Asquith to dine with us in our rooms on every day of the week, Sundays included. She would not have accepted, but that is another story.

However, I never did discover the real reason, and, as a matter of fact, there was no need to do so, for the Master's wife, in the interests of Liberalism, very kindly asked Mrs. Asquith to dinner herself. And so, that was how we dined, – the men in one building, the women in another, as closely segregated as though we had been members of some strict religious order which forbade the intermingling of the sexes.

Asquith was in great form at dinner. I had never seen him before, and if first impressions are of any value, be it recorded that he struck me as having a head far too large for his body. His face was of a pleasant, rosy hue, rather like that of a genial baby, his body was short and rather inclined to stoutness. Two things only about him suggested the sheather of swords – his hair and his voice. The former was long and white and so silky that one longed to stroke it. His voice was deep and rich with a quality that also suggested silk.

The first thing he said to me after we had been introduced was:

'Did you get my box?'

This cryptic remark needs a little explanation. As soon as Asquith had consented to speak for us he sent word by his secretary saying that it was most important that we should prepare for him a box, some ten inches high and twelve inches broad. This object must be covered in green baize, and placed on the table at which he was going to speak. It was destined, as we afterwards learnt, to carry his notes.

Such a request was, at first, a little surprising. One had always thought of Asquith as a man with an endless flow of language, who did not have to rely upon written memoranda in his speeches. However, the more one learns about apparently impromptu oratory the more does it appear in its true light, as carefully prepared. Winston Churchill has told us that the speech that gained him his greatest reputation as an impromptu was written out six times with his own hand. Bright used to have an entire synopsis hidden between the palm and fingers of his left hand, and I am sure the more 'mountainous' districts in Lloyd George's perorations are carefully hacked and hewn beforehand. So at least Asquith was in good company.

During dinner I asked him if it was true that he had once laughingly summarized the most valuable attribute of Balliol men as a 'tranquil consciousness of superiority.'

'A tranquil consciousness of *effortless* superiority,' he corrected. 'Don't forget the "effortless." That's the whole point of it. But,' he added, 'I don't want to corrupt the youth of Balliol by such agreeable theories as that.'

He had an extraordinary thirst for knowledge about post-war Oxford – a thirst that was almost pathetic, so clearly did it indicate a love of the very stuff, one might almost say, the very smell, of scholasticism. Was there much unrest among the undergraduates? Did they find it hard to settle down after the War? How many people were abandoning the classics? And wnat was their chief reason for doing so? Was it lack of time or lack of thought, or mere laziness? One could not help thinking what an admirable Master of Balliol Asquith would have made if he had ever chosen to abandon politics for university life – (his natural element).

Dinner passed quickly under this fusillade of questions, and I was longing to see how Mrs. Asquith had fared in her comparatively solitary dinner. It cannot have been a very inspiriting one, for when we all trooped over to the lodge, and joined them in the big room upstairs, the atmosphere was gloomy, not to say strained. Mrs. Asquith was sitting on a table, swinging her legs, which were encased in grey Russian top-boots, and she greeted our arrival with a whoop of delight, and started to talk very quickly, as though she had been pent up for years. How wonderful of the undergraduates to give her a bouquet of red roses! Had they guessed that she was going to wear a red hat? And did they mind her not dressing? No? How charming of one to say that she looked nice in anything, etc., etc.

The Master's wife, on the other hand, said nothing at all, but remained by the fireplace in what appeared to be deep melancholy. I went up to her and said, 'We really ought to be going along to the Town Hall now. The meeting starts in five minutes.'

At this she brightened considerably, and said:

'Is Mrs. Asquith going?'

I explained that it was snowing outside, and that the other guests had to be disposed of first. Mr. and Mrs. Asquith would bring up the rear, as they were the most important people.

'Oh, I see,' she said, 'Mrs. Asquith's the climax, is she?'

I was very thankful when we were all safely landed at the Town Hall, and the meeting had begun.

I needn't say anything about the meeting itself, except that everybody made admirable speeches, which called forth a great deal of applause, and set the fires of Liberalism blazing fervently. A few extra lines may, however, be inserted to make this sketch of Mrs. Asquith a little less shadowy.

I am perfectly certain that this lady has been very much maligned by the British public. A section of that public regards her as vulgar because she is enthusiastic, prejudiced because she is loyal, conceited because she is frank, and generally a very tiresome creature. They have not the wit to realize that she is, in reality, a woman almost unbearably sensitive, who is aggressive only in self-defence, and that she is so emotional that she does things in public which some people regard as outrageous only because they do not understand her.

I shall never forget, for example, seeing her at the end of the meeting, put her hand on her husband's shoulder while they were playing God Save the King, and, as soon as the King was saved, throwing the flowers from her bouquet into the stolid faces of the crowd below. How I sympathized with her at that moment. I should have liked to jump to the roof with elation. The only difference was that Mrs. Asquith had the courage to do what she wanted, and I hadn't.

CHAPTER SEVEN

*In which Mr. Winston Churchill loses his Temper, and Mr.
Horatio Bottomley wins his Debate*

You may, or you may not, have heard of the
Oxford Union Society. It has a habit of producing future Prime Ministers. Among its past
presidents it numbers such illustrious names as
Gladstone, Salisbury, Asquith, Birkenhead, etc., etc.,
to say nothing of such minor fry as occasional Arch-
bishops, diplomats and ambassadors.

Among its past presidents it also numbers myself.
A matter again of no importance, except for the
people with whom it brought me into touch.

Now, every president of the Oxford Union Society
can invite, during his term of office, not more than
two distinguished statesmen to address the Society.
As soon as I had been elected I looked round for
two men who might bring a little live blood into our
somewhat academic discussions, and there seemed
no better couple, for this purpose, than Winston
Churchill, the Secretary for War, and Horatio
Bottomley, M.P., who is at present languishing in
gaol. Both expressed themselves as delighted to
accept, and dates were fixed for their respective
appearances.

A terrible problem faced me as Winston's arrival
drew near. I had to give a dinner, not only to him,
but to his guests (four of them), and about a dozen
others. When one dines in this fashion, one has to
dine well, with Moët 1914 and all the usual things
which go to make good oratory. Being quite devoid
of funds, and having long before exhausted my
allowance in riotous living, there seemed no alter-

native but to make a descent on an already over-
burdened parent. Then suddenly, a charming
friend, who is now brightening a not very brilliant
House of Commons, suggested that we should all
dine with him . . . a suggestion which was carried
nem. con.

Winston was the first great English statesman
who ever dined with me (probably the last also).
Remembering that it was he who had, on his own
responsibility, given orders to the British Fleet at
the outset of the War which were probably instru-
mental in saving the Empire, I sat gazing at him in a
sort of awe. 'This,' I thought, 'is the face that
launched a thousand ships.' And yet there was
something a little incongruous about Winston
Churchill in this tiny room. He was so vigorous,
he breathed so hard, and spoke so quickly that one
feared he might at any moment seize all his knives
and forks and glasses and arrange them in the
form of a field of battle to illustrate his martial
theories.

This he actually did. I happened to mention that,
in order to help our memory of the campaigns of
Napoleon, I and several others who were working
together, had composed a series of rhymes round the
tributaries of the Po, which we found of the greatest
value.

That set Winston off. He seized a knife, a fork,
and a salt cellar and made with them a little plan
round which he marched the imaginary armies of
Napoleon. I have never heard anybody talk of war
with such gusto. With each martial adjective, a light
seemed to be turned on inside his head, his eyes

gleamed, his lips parted, and he talked so vividly that the slight impediment in his speech, which he has always so pluckily fought, was forgotten. And when he had finished he gave me an exhaustive list of military treatises on Napoleon, which, needless to say, I did not attempt to read.

Winston was a wonderful talker that night – not only of war, but of other arts, notably of literature and painting. He asked how long it had taken me to write my novel *Prelude*.

'I haven't the least idea,' I said, 'because it was done in bits and patches over a period of about five months.'

'Didn't you work at it regularly?'

'No. I don't see how you can do work in that manner if it is to have any sort of claim to be emotional.'

'Nonsense.'

I sat up, and Winston began to put forward some very interesting theories on the writing of books.

'You should go to your room every day at nine o'clock,' he said, 'and say to yourself, "I am going to sit here for four hours and write." '

'But suppose you *can't* write? Suppose you've got a headache, or indigestion. . . .'

'You've got to get over that. If you sit waiting for inspiration, you will sit there till you are an old man. Writing is a job like any other job, like marching an army for instance. If you sit down and wait till the weather is fine, you won't get very far with your troops. It's the same with writing. Discipline yourself. Kick yourself. Irritate yourself. But write. It's the only way.'

Advancing years have taught me that there is a good deal more than half of the truth in what Winston said. The ideal combination would seem to be a little of both spirits – the spirit that enabled Mozart to sit down, like an accountant, and write his divine melodies at his desk, and the spirit that urged Beethoven out into the woods and forests when the storm was at its height.

To return to Winston. He made a very good speech – (it was about Russia) – quite as good as those of the undergraduates who were opposing him – won his motion, and then trotted off to bed, with the cheers of a thousand young throats ringing in his ears.

The next day I called on him after breakfast and suggested that it might amuse him to walk round some of the colleges. 'All right,' he said, and we set out forthwith, while I tried to recall the names of the various buildings which one passed every day, but never recognized.

However, Winston strode along gloomily, smoking a cigar, tapping his stick on the pavement, and taking not the faintest notice of my chatter, which showed his good sense. Still, I wanted to know the reason for his ill-humour, and was about to ask him if he had got out of bed on the wrong side, when he said:

'There was a shorthand reporter there last night, of course?'

I shook my head. 'No. We don't run to that.

He glared at me in astonishment. 'But there was a man from the *Morning Post?*'

'Yes,' I said, 'but he only takes extracts. Did you want a report?'

'I should damned well think I did,' replied the Secretary for War. 'I said a lot of very — er — delicate things last night and it's most important for me to know what I *did* say.'

I remembered, with exquisite clarity, his remarks about footpads, assassins and other gentlemen with whom His Majesty's Government, of which he was a prominent member, were at that period negotiating. And I also appreciated the fact that he was honest enough to stand up for his personal convictions at the risk of being severely censured by his colleagues. However, there seemed nothing to be done.

'Perhaps,' I remarked, with singularly misplaced brightness, 'it may be a good thing in view of the delicacy of the discussion, that there *was* a certain vagueness about what you actually said?'

For reply, he merely clasped his hands behind his back, made a clucking noise with his teeth and said: 'Is that Lincoln or Exeter?'

That night, in the House of Commons, several indignant gentlemen rose to their feet to draw the attention of the House to the indiscretions of the Secretary for War at Oxford. Many uncomplimentary things were said before the matter was allowed to drop. For one night, at least, I experienced something of the thrill of government.

It is a long step from Winston Churchill to Horatio Bottomley, but not quite as long as might at first be imagined. Both men have a good deal in common — (this is meant as a tribute to Horatio rather than a reflection on Winston) — and if Horatio had been to Harrow instead of to a little school in the East End of London, it is not impossible that he would have risen to Cabinet rank, have stirred the nation with patriotic speeches, and have gone down to history as one of the great men of our times.

At any rate, he seemed to me a fascinating figure, and one who should enliven any debate in which he spoke.

I therefore wrote to him, suggesting that he might care to visit us. By return of post I received a reply, typed on the sort of notepaper that is described by stationers as 'superfine,' and couched in the third person. It stated that 'Mr. Bottomley considered himself honoured by the invitation, which he had great pleasure in accepting. Mr. Bottomley would also like to know the subject of the debate. If he had any say in the matter he would prefer to speak in favour of the Independent Political Party. Failing that, he would like to attack the League of Nations, which he considered a useless and a pernicious institution.' The Independent Party won the day.

On the night of Bottomley's arrival, I was suddenly sent into a panic by the news that a gang of undergraduates, who considered that the dignity of the Union was being outraged by including Bottomley among its 'distinguished visitors,' had arranged to kidnap him. The plan was to meet him at the station before anybody else could get near, to hurry him into a motor-car, and to drive straight up to Boar's Hill, where he would be given a good dinner, and allowed to depart in peace after the debate was over. I immediately went down to the station, seized several burly porters and informed them of the situ-

ation. Whether or no these measures had the effect
of nipping the plot in the bud, history will never
know. He arrived safely.

A grotesque figure, one would have said at first
sight. Short and uncommonly broad, he looked
almost gigantic in his thick fur coat. Lack-lustre
eyes, heavily pouched, glared from a square and
sallow face. He seemed to have a certain resentment
against the world at large. It was not till he began
to talk that the colour mottled his cheeks and the
heavy hues on his face were lightened.

Was there any excitement at his coming? Yes? He
smiled like a child. A lot of big men came down
to speak, didn't they? Asquith, Winston, Lloyd
George? Yes? 'And now, Horatio.' He rubbed his
coarse hands and chuckled.

At the entrance to the hotel he stood sunning
himself in such publicity as was afforded by the gap-
ing hall porter and his underlings. He stumped
across to the office, his fur coat swinging open, drew
from his pocket a heavy gold pen, and signed his
name with a flourish. The signature was illegible,
but the gesture was Napoleonic.

He dined with me that night, and kept the small
gathering of undergraduates I had invited in a constant splutter of unholy laughter. 'Do I pay my
income tax?' he said. 'Not I.' And he told us, with
a dazzling display of figures, exactly how he managed to avoid that obligation. To my dying day I
shall regret that I forget his method. He discussed
religion, with his tongue well out in his cheek. He
drew for us a little portrait gallery of contemporary
politicians, as crude but as vivid as the work of an

inspired pavement artist. Birkenhead seemed to be the sole politician for whom he entertained any genuine regard.

'When Birkenhead was seriously ill a few months ago,' he said, 'I was the only man he allowed into his room. I would go and sit with him for hours, sometimes talking, sometimes just silent. Funny isn't it?'

We adjourned to the debating hall, were greeted with uproarious applause, took our places. As the debate proceeded, I looked from time to time at Bottomley. He seemed, suddenly, to have grown nervous. His face was flushed and hot, and from time to time he mopped his forehead with a large silk handkerchief. The light and airy chatter, the brilliant irrelevancies, of the Oxford Union seemed to be filling him with a certain mistrust. He had never known an audience like this. Every phrase, every gesture, he watched with narrowed eyes, leaning forward intently. And then he rose to speak. He took the wind out of our sails from the very beginning.

I had been afraid that before this, 'the most critical audience in the world,' he would try to assume an air of culture that was foreign to him, that he would endeavour to put on airs. He did exactly the reverse. After his opening sentence there was a moment when everything hung in the balance. He made some rather inapt historical reference, paused, and was for a moment at a loss. And then, quite calmly and deliberately, he looked round and said:

'Gentlemen: I have not had your advantages. What poor education I have received has been gained in the University of Life.'

Dead silence. I sat back, marvelling at the consummate stagecraft of the man. After that brief remark, any men who laughed at his pronunciation or his mannerism would be cads, and they knew it. And he knew that they knew it.

From that moment, he sailed on triumphantly. His eloquence was uncanny. For sheer force of oratory I have never heard anyone like him. Compared with him, Asquith was a dry stick. (I am talking of the manner, not of the matter.) And his aptness of retort was modelled on the best Union styles. For instance, he happened to use, during one of his passages, the phrase 'the right to work.' A Welsh miner who was in the gallery, and who was, as usual, on strike, cried out ironically, "'ear, 'ear.'

Bottomley did not look at him. He merely added, in exactly the same voice as he had used before, 'a right which I am sure we will gladly grant to the honourable member.' Delicious.

Nor was his repartee merely flippant. One of the preceding speakers had made a great hit by referring to him, somewhat contemptuously, as 'a voice crying in the wilderness.' Bottomley took up the gage and hurled it with unerring skill back into the face of his opponent. 'All my life,' he cried, 'I have been a voice crying in the wilderness. All my life I have battled alone, fought alone, struggled for causes that other men have deserted as hopeless. A voice crying in the wilderness! Yes, gentlemen, and I am proud of it!' Thunders of applause.

He won his motion by several hundred votes, and when he left the hall, they cheered him to the echo. But he did not seem particularly elated by his success. When he returned to a party I gave for him at my rooms afterwards, the voting had totalled about 1,100 – a few less than a record attendance. 'I'd hoped I should draw the biggest house you ever had,' he said with a sigh. 'Are you sure there was no mistake in the counting?'

I assured him that the tellers were thoroughly trustworthy.

He nodded. 'Well, it can't be helped. Still – it's a pity.'

Further regrets were stopped by the discovery that nobody could open any of the champagne. 'Give me a bottle,' said Bottomley. 'I'll show you a trick.'

He seized a bottle in his podgy hand, went to the door, half opened it, shut it again, gave the bottle a pull, and lo! – the cork was removed. As he drank our healths he looked across and said 'Damned fine champagne.'

He was either a liar or a very bad judge of champagne, for it was the worst wine I have ever tasted.

We had arranged to breakfast together the next morning, and at nine o'clock I arrived at the hotel. It was a drizzling, dreary sort of morning, with a cold wind, and an indeterminate mist over the roofs. Bottomley came downstairs looking very tired. The lustre had faded from the heavy eyes, the bulky frame had lost all elasticity.

'And what would you like for breakfast?' I asked him.

He protruded the tip of his tongue, paused, and then gave me a wink. All Whitechapel was in that wink.

'A couple of kippers,' he said, 'and a nice brandy and soda.'

I gave the order, as gravely as possible, to the waiter, and watched him gulp his brandy, leaving the kippers untouched. He cheered up after that, and by the time his cab had arrived he was quite gay. 'I've enjoyed myself,' he said to me when I bade him good-bye. 'Enjoyed myself like hell.'

It will need a clever man to write *finis* to an analysis of the character of Horatio Bottomley — part genius, part scoundrel, and yet, wholly human.

CHAPTER EIGHT

Being an Impression of Two Ladies of Genius

So far the feminine element has not obtruded greatly into these pages, not for lack of females, but for lack of distinguished ones. It is a matter of little significance to the reader that in May I met a charming girl called Jean, and in June lost my heart to a languorous beauty named Helen. But at about this time (the summer of 1920) I did meet and get to know two very remarkable women.

The first was Mrs. Patrick Campbell. She was staying at a house whither I journeyed in late July to escape the heat of a London summer. My first sight of her was as I emerged from the car; very dirty and dishevelled after a long journey, in which somebody had spilt a bottle of champagne all over my trousers. I entered the hall, and observed a strange, dark woman in orange looking at me, wondered who she was, wondered still more when she advanced and said in a deep booming voice:

'Oh, young man. Run upstairs quickly before you go in to see them. The room is full of earls and cocktails.'

This remarkable announcement (which was true in so far as there was an earl somewhere in the distance, and the clinking of ice in glasses) was followed by a mutual introduction.

A fiery, billowing, passionate, discontented creature of genius – that is my impression of Mrs. Patrick Campbell. She absolutely dominated the party during my whole visit. I fell passionately in love with her, with the shy, ridiculous love of twenty-one for –?

Try to see her as I see her now. The tall, cool dining-room, the Romney smiling from the wall, the long dining-table, and, near the end, Mrs. Patrick Campbell, hunched up, scowling, smoking a cigar, and as she puffed the smoke into the face of the lady opposite (whom she detested) telling the following story:

'Do you know' (oh! the mellow boom of that magical voice!) 'the story of the old hen that was crossing the road and that was run over by a Rolls-Royce? There was a flutter of feathers, a shrill cackle and then —' (turning to her neighbour) 'what do you think the hen said as she died? *My God, what a rooster!*'

I don't think anybody was ever quite so rude to people as Mrs. Patrick Campbell. She would stand in front of the glass, tugging fitfully at her dress, and then, with her head on one side, she would say, in dreamy but resounding tones:

'Isn't it awful? I try to look like a lady and all I look like is Miss —.' The fact that Miss — was standing just behind her, made no difference at all.

At this house there was a swimming bath — rather on the Roman model, with pillars of pale blue marble mosaic, and little nooks and corners where one could drink cocktails before summoning up the energy to dive in. It was a very hot summer and the bath was in great demand, especially after tennis. On one of these occasions we all assembled, in dressing-gowns of varying gorgeousness, and plunged into the water. Enter Mrs. Patrick Campbell. She herself was in a tea-gown, having no intention of bathing. Lying on a couch, she surveyed the splashing throng. Suddenly, as a pretty girl in a *décolletée* bathing dress scrambled up on the diving board the great voice rang out:

'I'm sure you wouldn't appear like that before the man you loved!'

I don't know what happened. I only know that the two never spoke to one another again.

And yet, when one got her by herself, she was the most fascinating of creatures. She was, at the time, moving into a little house near by, and whenever the opportunity occurred, we would go over to assist her in her task. It is probable that the ' assist-ance' considerably delayed her entry into possession, for though we had all of us very decided ideas upon house decoration, we had not the remotest idea of how to carry them out. I remember standing in a small and dishevelled room for nearly an hour, while we all argued exactly where a set of the works of Bernard Shaw (which the author had given her) should be placed. Finally, with a gesture that would have done credit to an empress, Mrs. Patrick Campbell swept the whole lot on to the floor, drew from her pocket the manuscript of a one-act melodrama by Clemence Dane, and tramped round the room reciting it, her golden voice echoing over the empty house. She must have quite demoralized the young man who was putting in a new bath, and she certainly created havoc among the various vases and oddments with which the floor was strewn.

After that, we decided that we would leave the house to itself for an hour or two, and go into the village to buy garden implements. I wish you could have seen Mrs. Patrick Campbell stalking into that provincial ironmonger's shop. She stood in the entrance, drawing her furs around her, swept out her hand and pointed to some extraordinary instrument covered with knobs and spikes (probably designed for the uprooting of turnips).

'What,' she boomed, 'is that?'

The man, like a startled rabbit, tried to give her some indication of its use.

'Give it to me,' she cried.

The next thing was a rake. She asked for a r-r-rake, rolling her r's and her eyes as though she were asking for some esoteric poison. When she held the rake at arm's length she reminded one irresistibly of a Britannia of the decadence. Choppers, trowels, insecticide, squirting things – enough to staff a place four times the size of her own – were all ordered and bundled into the car, so that when eventually we set out for home we must have looked like a party of *sans-culottes* departing to arm their local legion.

The actual use of these instruments was never fully discovered. The rake was of course a simple matter, and was employed with great aplomb in removing the remaining gravel from the centre of the drive to the sides, where it served as a very effectual choker of the drains. The clippers also wrought confusion with the grass borders, and became caked with earth and grit. But the spiked thing remained a complete mystery.

I never understood how Mrs. Patrick Campbell wrote her autobiography. When I saw her it was apparently due at the publishers towards the end of the next month, although not a word of it had been written. She would suddenly get up in the middle of a conversation, and rush away to her room saying, 'Now, I am going to write.' But half an hour later she would invariably be back again, booming at us from the sofa.

This habit of leaving things to the last moment undoubtedly explains, to a large extent, the fact that her later career has not been marked with the same triumph as she enjoyed during her earlier years, in spite of the fact that she is still the superb genius, shining with a dark radiance that hardly any of her younger rivals possesses.

Does she allow that genius to run to waste? I wonder. She does not appear to have the capacity for taking pains. Philip Moeller, the author of *George Sand*, told me that she was anything but word-perfect in the title-rôle. 'At the final dress rehearsal,' he said, 'she was sweeping about the stage with the text in her hand, reading it, word by word. She carried it off somehow, by gagging – magnificent gagging, if you like – but still, you can't expect to play a part on those lines.'

A pity, a decided pity. For so fine and sensitive an artist must have suffered tortures when she first saw inferior artists taking her place. And when she had to appear at the music-halls it must have been like putting a queen in a pillory. I once heard a marvellous story of her in this connection.

It is alleged to have occurred at some London music-hall where – sadly to relate – she had to share the honours with some performing sea-lions. Think of it! Mrs. Patrick Campbell, who had swept London off its feet in *The Second Mrs. Tanqueray*, having to appear in the unworthy company of beasts of that nature, which probably eat their young and sleep all the winter. These animals were apparently incapable of appreciating true art, for during the whole of her act (which preceded their own), they made the most appalling noises off stage, booming and bellowing for food. They were, of course, kept hungry in order that they might go through their tricks with proper alacrity.

Mrs. Patrick Campbell, according to the story, put up with the sea-lions for two performances, but after that, she had had enough. On the following evening she therefore paid an early visit to the theatre, a strange bundle under her arm. In this bundle was a packet of succulent fish with which she proceeded to feed the sea-lions one by one, addressing them, as she did so, in terms of great affection. After a couple of fish the bellowing ceased, and gave way to contented licking of lips. . . .

Mrs. Patrick Campbell went through her act in a deathly silence that night. But when the sea-lions came on, the general impression of the audience was that it was a very poor show.

I cannot better introduce the other lady who at this time so impressed me than by quoting a very penetrating sentence that was written about one of her books by Mr. Middleton Murry. It referred to *Vera* (by the authoress of *Elizabeth and Her German Garden*), and he called it 'A Wuthering Heights written by a Jane Austen.'

For Lady Russell – if one may be so unkind as to strip from her the mask of anonymity which she is always so careful to preserve – is just like that. It is as though she dwelt in an early Victorian drawing-room, listening to some passionate dialogue of life that was being carried on outside the window. The voices rise and fall, the rain splashes against the bright panes, the wind moans and whistles round the stoutly built walls. Then, there is a lull, and in the silence may be heard the scratching of her little quill pen, transcribing the violent things she has heard in a tiny, spidery handwriting, catching the thunder in a polished phrase. And when she has finished writing, there, on the paper, is a story as full of tension, fierce and frightening as any that dwells in the broken, passionate sentences of Emily Brontë.

When one meets her, inevitably she suggests Dresden China, with her tiny voice, tiny hands, tiny face, tiny manners. And then suddenly, with a shock, you realize that the Dresden China is hollow, and is filled with gunpowder. Not that Lady Russell will tell you. You simply sense it, and stand back a little, wondering.

After I had returned to London, I was trying to endure one of those dull Septembers which seem to concentrate in themselves all the heat and stuffiness of a summer that has outstayed its welcome, when somebody rang up and said, 'Come to lunch. I want you to meet a very charming lady.'

I went to lunch, and there were certainly several very charming ladies, but one knew them all before. Until, twenty minutes late, the door opened, and a

...e with blue eyes floated across the floor
...forgive me, will yiu? I feel I must be
... then everything was changed.

...e really ought to be some sort of musical
...otation for giving the exact timbre of people's
voices. Lady Russell's is a delicious voice, like a
dove that has become slightly demoralized by perch-
ing too long on a French hat. Her 'U' sounds are
startlingly French, and yiu, pronounced *à la fran-
çaise*, is the only way you can write it. She does not
really talk, she croons aloud. And here again, one
comes up against the Austen-Brontë combination.
No other woman could possibly deliver herself of
such remarks in so utterly dulcet a tone.

It was at the time when her (?) book *In the Mountains* was being so well reviewed, and there was just
enough doubt as to whether she really had written
it to lend piquancy to the discussion.

'In the Mountains?' she said. 'It sounds like a
Bliu Guide.'

'You wrote it — you *know* you wrote it.'

'*Yiu* may know I wrote it. I haven't even read it.
But if *yiu* like it, it must be improper. So I shan't
read it.'

She swore till the very last that she did not write
it.

'I couldn't have written it, could I, because I only
published a book last year, and I write terribly
slowly. Scratch out all the time. I want to write a
play.'

'Why don't you?'

She sighed. 'It's so difficult to know what's going
to happen to a play. Yiu always know with a novel

that it will be published, but with a play yiu never know, du yiu? I once had a play produced and I was so thrilled that I used to go every night and sit all by myself in the pit, thinking "What a clever girl am I." But I think the little man at the door began to think I must be in love with him and so I stopped. And so did the play.'

Suddenly – (this was after lunch) – 'Let's write a play *now*.'

'What sort of a play?'

'A play with heaps and heaps of tiny scenes, all lasting only about five minutes. With Bach fugues in between. Beautifully lit. Tiny tragedies. Tiny comedies. Like the things that happen in one's life. Some of the plays might be silent. And then – oh, *du* lets' – and then after each funny little emotion, one would always have the fugue to recall one back to life.'

It sounds a fascinating idea, and I wish she would do it. Perhaps she will. So that if ever a unique entertainment by an anonymous writer is produced in London, of the type sketched above, you will know who is responsible for it.

Lady Russell has her own way of administering criticism to bad writers – the sort of way which makes one swear never to do it again. In one of my novels, which she had read, there comes a passage of a very lurid and foolish nature, where a villainous vicar strikes an adventuress across the face. One develops fairly quickly, and I knew, almost as soon as the book was published, that this passage was rotten stuff I met Lady Russell shortly after she read it and she said, 'I *du* like your book And I

loved the bad old man who hit the girl on the mouth.'
Silence. Utter silence. And then a laugh. I went
straight home and threw that silly novel into the fire.

But that is not nearly so damning as she can be.
I shall never forget my thrill of delight when I heard
of her quite classic rebuke to one of the world's most
tiresome women. The scene had better remain
veiled in mystery, but one can say that she had
several amusing people staying with her. There
suddenly arrived in the neighbourhood Lady –,
who, as everybody who knows her will tell you, will
go miles in any weather to be near a celebrity. She
was full of her latest discovery, a very decorative
young soldier, who had won far more than his share
of medals in the war. Lady – talked about him
till everybody felt inclined to scream: how she had
lunched with him in Paris, how he had done this,
that and the other. 'And do you know,' she added,
in a vibrating voice, 'he was wounded in sixteen
places!'

Lady Russell looked at her with a plaintive smile.
'I didn't know men *had* so many places,' she said.

It would be interesting to know what she really
thought of life, or failing that, what she really
thought of her own work, but very few people have
ever managed to get behind the mask of anonymity,
and they all come back with different stories of what
they have seen. One thing I do know, and that is
that *Vera had* to be written. The terrible brute of a
man, the feeling of suspense which hangs over the
pages like a menace – they were as inevitable as a
human birth.

'Did you like writing that book?' I asked her once,

'I hated it,' she said, in a whisper. And then, looking down at the floor, 'Isn't he a brute? An absolute brute? Have you ever known anybody so horrible?' She shuddered as though she were talking of a very real person.

Whatever one may say of her, the fact remains that she occupies a place in modern literature that is unique, because to the public she is only a pen, and not a person. When they think of anybody like Sheila Kaye-Smith, they call to mind bobbed hair, black eyebrows, and a cottage on the Sussex downs. When they think (as they apparently sometimes do) of Hall Caine, they call up visions of a beard, private suites at the Savoy, and countless mysterious legends of his doings in the Isle of Man. When they hear of Stephen McKenna it is always with the knowledge that he has either just been to or returned from the West Indies and is either going or has gone to some party or other in London. But they never think at all of Lady Russell, because they simply do not know she exists. They are caught up in the fascination of her work, they wonder for a moment what manner of man or woman produced it. And all they have to guide them is a blank title-page.

CHAPTER NINE

In which We Meet a Ghost

A<small>T</small> this point in the narrative it seems fitting to introduce a spiritual element which, up to the moment, has not been very noticeable.

You may have seen, two Christmases ago, a sensational article in The *Weekly Dispatch*, by one Lord St. Audries, telling of a ghostly midnight adventure which he had experienced with two friends in a Devonshire house. The article made something of a sensation at the time. The *Daily Mail* devoted a leading article to the subject, and many American papers quoted it in full. The full story of that adventure, however, has never been told. And since the two other conspirators mentioned in the article were my brother and myself, it seems that the time has now come when the true story of that very remarkable evening may be told in full.

It was the first week in June when Peter — as it is shorter to call him — came down, and it was in the third week in June that the thing happened. In case you might imagine that the atmosphere of my home was favourable to ghosts, it is necessary to state that we had lived, during those two intervening weeks, the most distressingly healthy of lives. Most of my mornings had been spent in wrestling with the foreign policy of Queen Elizabeth or the political theories of Mr. Aristotle, a task that was not made any the more pleasant by the thud, thud of tennis balls which came from the lawns below. But in the afternoon we would always set out together, sometimes to motor up to Dartmoor and picnic in heather, but more often down to the sea, where we bathed, and spent the long hot afternoons lazing about on the beach.

One Sunday – the last Sunday of Peter's visit – we all went to evensong. It was a glorious evening when, at about seven o'clock, we came out of church, and we decided to walk home, taking the short cut by the road over the hill. This road, I may say, runs straight from the church, past various houses, until it reaches the gates which guard the approach to our own home.

A full moon hung over the hills – a little pale in the fresh light of dusk – and after we had been walking a few minutes, Peter stopped, looked over a wall and said:

'What a fearful house.'

We looked with him. It was a house which I will call Weir. It had been untenanted for nearly thirty years and was falling to rack and ruin. The roof had long ago disappeared, the paint was peeling from the faded green shutters, and as we looked a bat flew out of one of the second-story windows, showing that the glass had also vanished.

'Why has it been allowed to get like that?' asked Peter.

'Haunted,' said my brother. 'At least, that's the legend.' And then he told him how nobody could ever live in it, how strange sounds, screams and the pattering of hurried feet were heard by passers-by, how it was narrated that in years gone by there had been a terrible murder there, in fact, all the usual things which are told in Christmas numbers of popular magazines.

Peter interrupted him.

'I'm for going in,' he said.

'What on earth for? You don't believe in ghosts, do you?'

'No. Nor disbelieve in them. But, it would be rather fun.'

And that was how it began, and how we found ourselves, three hours later, walking back over the road by which we had come.

The road was quite deserted, for the town went to bed at early hours, and as we swung along, wearing our flannels, for it was a hot night, I took a certain interest in the state of mind of my two companions. My brother was, frankly, a little on edge. He had a candle in one pocket, and a crucifix in the other, to meet the respective powers of darkness with which we might be confronted. Peter was just – how shall I say? – alert. He had had experiences which might be described as psychical in the past, and he was more or less prepared for anything that might happen. And I was just enjoying the whole thing, quite confident that we should see nothing at all, but none the less amused by the possibility that, perhaps, if we were lucky . . .

We clambered over the wall, for the gate was locked, walked down some steps, through some bushes, and round to the front of the house. It stood about thirty yards back from the road, and the main grounds stretched out in front. As it was built on sloping ground, the tangled grass and shrubberies in front were on a level with the basement, through which we had to enter. The first floor was on a level with the road behind us.

It was an absolutely still night, so still that the

poplar trees behind us were etched against the moon in a motionless trelliswork of silver leaves.

'Come on,' said Peter. We decided to enter the house through one of the windows in front of us. The glass was broken, and there was no difficulty in raising the sash. We opened the window and as soon as we had done so, it fell down again with a bang. The sash had long ago rotted.

'Give me your stick,' said my brother. 'I'll prop this thing up. We might have to come out in a hurry, and we don't want to crash into a lot of broken glass.'

I gave him the stick, and he wedged the window firmly into position. It is lucky that he did so.

We clambered in one by one, groping our way in the semi-darkness. As soon as the candle was lit, a room of indescribable melancholy flickered into view. The plaster had fallen in great lumps from the ceiling, so that we walked with a crunching noise that echoed all over the house. Wooden boxes and planks strewed the floor. The wall-paper had almost all peeled from the walls, though some of it still clung in strips, like pieces of decaying skin.

'Where?' said Peter.

'Upstairs, I think – don't you?'

'Right.'

We spoke in whispers, as though afraid of disturbing something that might be lying asleep above, and one by one made our way up a narrow twisting staircase that led into the main hall.

In this hall we paused, undetermined where to go next. Right before us was the front door, and on the left, the two principal rooms of the house. Both of their doors were open, and through them one caught sight of a floor on to which the moonlight poured abundantly. To the right was a corridor leading to some rooms that were shrouded in darkness. Just by us was the continuation of the staircase, which in the old days had led up to the rooms above, but which now led (after turning a corner beyond which we could not see) straight up to the sky.

We began to make a tour of the house, and chose, firstly, one of the big rooms on the left. There was hardly any need for a candle here, since the moonlight was so brilliant, but we took it for the sake of dark corners. We found absolutely nothing. Only a big, silent room, looking out on to the garden, with a single cupboard, which was empty. A most prosaic room it must have been in daylight, and even now, there was nothing particularly alarming about it.

'So far, so good,' said my brother.

'Let's try the other room now,' I said.

I went outside, and stood in the hall, waiting for them to follow. I was not feeling 'creepy,' although I should not in the least mind admitting it. As a matter of fact, I was rather disappointed that nothing had happened. I stood there waiting, looking into the darkness of the corridor on the right.

And then suddenly, the first alarm. It was not in the least the most important thing that happened that night, but since it happened to me, I take a particular interest in it.

As I stood there, I was thinking in the odd, inconsequent way in which one does think, of an essay which I had been writing that morning, when suddenly I thought – 'I am thinking very slowly. My brain does not seem to be working properly.' And then, with a thrill of dismay I realized that exactly the same physical process was taking place in my head as takes place on those dreary occasions when I have been forced to have an anæsthetic. The left side of the brain starts to be covered with a black film (almost like the shutter of a camera), which gradually closes over, from left to right. While this is going on I can think perfectly clearly with the right side. Thought and consciousness do not cease until the film has closed completely over. Then, everything is blackness.

This was now happening to me, but with two differences. The film was spreading over my brain far more quickly, and the agent which was responsible for it was not an anæsthetic but a force which I can only describe as a form of suction, coming very distinctly from a room down the corridor on the right.

'Hullo! What's up?'

I saw them standing before me. With every effort of concentration, I managed to say, in an absurdly stilted voice: 'The candle. Quick, the candle. Outside.' I found the candle placed in my hand. My feet carried me downstairs, I half fell to the window, and then – the film closed over.

A minute later I found myself sitting up on the grass, feeling absolutely normal again, though strangely tired. What had happened? It was exceedingly difficult to say. Nothing – and yet, everything.

All I knew was, that here in the garden I was safe. But inside . . .

'I wish to goodness you wouldn't go in again,' I said.

However, they were now more determined than ever to make a thorough investigation, and after waiting to see that I was all right, they clambered once more through the window.

Not one corner, not one crevice of that house did they leave unexamined. It was a very simple house to explore, because apart from the fact that the only possible entrance was by this particular window, the rooms themselves were square and stoutly built, and there were but few cupboards, and absolutely no mysterious closets or any other contrivances which might be thought to harbour 'ghosts,' or even, failing a ghost, a harmless tramp.

They spent about twenty-five minutes over their examination, and came out reporting that they had been everywhere — including the little room from which I had felt the 'influence,' and had found absolutely nothing.

'And now,' said Peter, 'I'm going in *alone*.'

'Alone? Good Lord, man, haven't you had enough of this business?'

He shook his head. 'No. I believe Paul's an "anti-influence." Sort of lightning conductor. He keeps them off. Perhaps it's the crucifix,' he laughed. 'Anyway, you remember that nothing happened to you until you went out in the hall away from him. And nothing happened to me, perhaps because we were together all the time.'

We tried to persuade him not to go. But he insisted, and we let him go in on the condition that he should take the candle, and that we should whistle to him every few minutes, while he would whistle back, to show that he was still there.

Once more, for the third time, he went into that house, while we sat down on the grass and listened to the sound of his footsteps as he clambered up the stairs. We heard him walk across the hall and sit down, as I judged, on the bottom of the steps, waiting. Then there came a faint whistle, and we whistled back.

Silence. We whistled again, and the answering echo sounded clearly. Another whistle, another answer. And so the minutes passed away.

Then — terror!

It was about twenty minutes after Peter had climbed through the window, and nothing had happened. The last whistle we had heard, which was about two minutes before, had been particularly shrill and cheerful. It seemed quite evident that we had drawn a blank, and I turned to my brother to suggest that we should call Peter out, and go home.

But, over our heads there came something which was not a sound, for there was no sound; not a wind, for the trees were still; nothing visible, for we saw nothing. A second later, a cry from the house, in Peter's voice, the like of which I hope I shall never hear again. It was a long-drawn ah-h-h! The sort of cry that a man would give who had been stabbed in the back.

We sprang to our feet, and rushed to the window. As we did so, a single cloud which had long been drifting slowly to the moon, started to obscure the light. Clambering through, we found ourselves in utter darkness. The planks and boxes which, by candlelight had been so easy to surmount, appeared gigantic. To add to the distraction there came from upstairs the wildest thuds and crashes, as though several men were struggling together.

'For God's sake, matches.'

'Haven't got any.'

'We must get some.'

We scrambled to the patch of light made by the window, rushed through the bushes, the noise of the struggle inside increasing all the time, vaulted the wall into the garden of the house next door, whose occupants were fortunately well known to us, pushed wide the front door which was fortunately open, seized a lantern which, by a miracle lay just inside the hall, tore back again, over the wall. As we vaulted the wall we heard a noise which was like a whole platoon of men stumbling down the stairs.

And then, 'Oh, my God!' in Peter's voice.

We met him as he emerged, staggering round the corner, his face dead white, his hair, his hands and his clothes covered with plaster and dirt. We took him into the next house, dosed him with brandy, and listened to the following story:

'When I got into the house,' said Peter, taking a plentiful gulp of brandy, 'I couldn't at first decide where to take up a position. I eventually chose the bottom of the staircase, for two reasons. It was central — that is to say, it commanded a view of nearly every door on the ground floor, and it also allowed me to face the corridor on to which opened the little

room from which you' (turning to me) 'felt the influence coming.

'I wasn't particularly hopeful of seeing anything.
However, something seemed to tell me that if there
were to be any manifestations, that is to say, quite
crudely, if there was a ghost, the centre of its activity
would be in that little room. My attention seemed
constantly switched in that direction, and after a few
minutes I sat quite still, my eyes fixed on the door
of the little room, which I could just make out as a
patch of greyish light in the darkness of the corridor.

'The minutes sped by, bringing nothing with them.
I heard your whistles outside. I whistled back. And
though the echo of my whistle sounded a little
uncanny in the lonely house, I still didn't feel in the
least "ghostly." I felt extraordinarily matter of fact.
I remember even wondering if the wood on which I
was sitting was damp.

'I suppose that about twenty minutes must have
gone by like this, and I was seriously thinking of
giving it up as a bad job. Your last whistle had
just sounded, and, growing impatient, I began to
rise to my feet, intending to have a final look at the
little room, and then to go home.

'Then, the thing happened. Out of that room,
down the darkness of the corridor, something rushed.
I don't know what it was, except that it was black,
and seemed to be shaped like a man. But two things
I did notice. The first was that I could see no face –
only blackness. The second was that it made no
noise. It rushed towards me over that bare floor
without a sound.

'I must have taken in those two facts subconsciously, for I had only two or three seconds in which to think. After that I was knocked flat on my back by some overwhelming force. I had a sickening, overwhelming sensation of evil, as though I were struggling with something beastly, out of hell.

'After that I remember struggling – it seemed to me for my life – staggering with an incredible effort to my feet – and fighting my way downstairs. If one's sensations in moments of half-consciousness are of any value, then I must have been fighting not with one thing, but with two or three. How I managed to get down the stairs, God knows. There was nothing but darkness and a hundred filthy influences sapping my strength. The next thing I remember is meeting you outside.'

Before I go on to the sequel to this story, just let me remind you of two things. Peter was, once again, a perfectly normal and healthy creature, going through the war like any other young man, fond of country life, the reverse of neurotic. Secondly, whatever it was that knocked him down, it was not a human being. That room from which the 'thing' emerged was empty. It had no cupboards, no secret doors. There was no possible way of entering it.

The sequel is as follows. We were naturally very anxious, after this exceedingly unpleasant experience, to find out a little more about Weir, and its antecedents, and with this object we paid a visit to a certain very charming lady who lived close by and who had an international reputation in things psychic. She knew all about it. She heard our story quite calmly, and without the least surprise.

'But do you mean to say,' she said, when we had finished, 'that you didn't *know?*'

'Didn't know what?' I asked impatiently.

And then it transpired that some forty years ago, Weir had been the scene of a particularly brutal double murder, in which a semi-insane doctor had done to death first his wife, and then a maid-servant. The actual scene of the murder was in the bathroom. *And the bathroom was the little room at the end of the corridor from which I had felt the influence coming and from which the thing had rushed at Peter.*

I could tell you a lot more about Weir if I had time — how when it was renovated, and re-inhabited a short time ago, no door in the place would keep shut, and how even the stodgiest tenants were forced to admit that something very devilish was on foot. How no dog can be got past the house after a certain hour. How — but one might go on like that for ever, and so I shall leave the facts as they stand.

Before leaving this question of ghosts, however, I cannot refrain from telling another story of the same kind, which also had Peter as its main victim. You may disbelieve it or not as you choose, but at least, even if you decide to treat it as pure fiction, it makes very good reading. And it is, as a matter of fact, the unadulterated truth.

The scene was laid about six years ago at St. Audries, a rambling, pleasant old place in Somersetshire. Peter had come home from London the night before, and apart from his sister, there was nobody there except the servants. On the second night, he was rather tired, and so at about ten o'clock he went to his room, which lay at the end of a long wing, a good distance away from the main body of the house. By half-past ten he was sound asleep.

Some hours later, in the middle of the night, he suddenly found himself awake, with that strange feeling that one has been disturbed by some noise outside. He rubbed his eyes, and sat up. Yes – distinctly there was a noise in the corridor. Wondering who on earth it could be at this time of night, he called out. There was no answer. Called again. Still no answer. Mystified, he rose from bed, put on a dressing-gown, and opened the door.

Outside, there was an old woman with a candle, standing a few yards away from him, regarding him with calm, wide eyes. He had never seen her before, and he spoke to her. She did not reply.

He then took a step towards her, and as he did so, she suddenly turned and began to walk away. Exceedingly curious, he began to follow, but she broke into a run. He too started running, and he chased her down corridors, along passages, up little staircases, faster and faster.

Suddenly at the other end of the house, when he was only a few yards behind, she turned into a corridor that led to a room from which there was no escape. There was the sound of a door slamming, and a second later he flung it open. Bright moonlight flooded the room. It was empty, silent, deserted.

Peter stood there, wondering. The only exit to

the room was by the door through which she had just entered. Unless of course one jumped out of the window, from which there was a sheer drop of forty feet on to a hard lawn. But the window was locked and barred. Nobody had opened it for years.

Shrugging his shoulders, he walked back to his room, a little disturbed, and greatly puzzled. Before he turned out the light to go to sleep again he glanced at his watch. It was two minutes to one.

The next morning, the whole adventure seemed so fantastic that he decided to say nothing about it. He therefore went down to breakfast, talked quite normally and cheerfully, and kept his peace.

As he rose to go out, his sister suddenly said to him:

'Oh, Peter. The clock on the mantelpiece has stopped, and it's a terrible nuisance to wind. What is the right time?'

Peter looked at the clock. It registered two minutes to one. He took out his own watch. That also marked two minutes to one.

'I'm not sure,' he said. 'I'll go outside and tell you.'

But in the hall the same thing had happened. The grandfather clock, which was usually kept fast, had also ceased ticking – at two minutes to one. The clocks in all the other rooms had stopped – at two minutes to one. Even a clock over the staircase, which could only be reached by a ladder, and of which he alone held the key, had stopped at two minutes to one.

That is all. There is no explanation, no 'sequel' of any kind. It just happened. It has never happened again.

Since these events I have looked the other way whenever I have seen any spiritualists coming down the street.

CHAPTER TEN

In which I Journey to Greece

IT was not easy, in the unrest and turmoil of the year 1921, for any young man to settle down to a definite occupation. There was a great outpouring from Oxford in that year, mainly consisting of those who had been to the war, had returned to the University to finish their studies, and had taken the shortened course. Men of that type, prematurely matured, seemed indeed to many of us, quite middle-aged, though most of them were not twenty-eight. And naturally having already lived many lives and died many deaths, the prospect of beginning all over again and being treated like children was not altogether pleasing.

Everybody who has done much public speaking at the University is always told that he ought to go to the Bar. It seems destined for him, as something almost inevitable – why, I could never quite understand, because mere eloquence is not nearly so great an asset at the Bar as the capacity to spurn delights, to live laborious days, and to make up your mind that for several years at least you must be content to be a very dull dog indeed.

I, too, was caught in this spirit of unrest. I went to London in search of a job, had no idea how to set about it, wrote odd articles, spent all my money, and returned home. Something had to be done, so I sat down and occupied the next four months in writing *Patchwork*, a novel of the new Oxford. It was published in the autumn, had a certain *succès d'estime*, and brought me in about enough money to pay my tailor's bill.

And then one day, there came a letter which set my heart beating quickly and filled me with a sense of adventure which made life seem more than worth living again. It was from my publishers, and it told me the following story:

A new revolution, it seemed, was on the point of breaking out in Greece. That unfortunate country was in the direst distress, being ruled by a monarch (the late King Constantine) who was not recognized by the Allies, who had already been exiled once, and who, unless drastic measures were taken, would be exiled again. The national exchequer was empty, the national spirit almost broken, and the national manhood practically exhausted by the war against Turkey, which had already lasted, on and off, for seven years.

The only way in which Greece could be saved was by the recognition of King Constantine by the Allies. Such an event was, at the moment, out of the question, since 'Tino' was regarded in France and England and America as an Arch-Traitor, a sort of miniature Kaiser, who by his treachery and his double dealing had imperilled our cause throughout the whole of the Near East.

But that legend of Tino, it was now alleged, was false. It had been carefully built up, during the war, by interested agents, on a fabric of complete falsehoods. The astounding nature of these falsehoods was contained in a collection of documents which was being carefully guarded. In those documents was material for a book which would cause a sensation throughout Europe as soon as it was published.

Would I go to Athens and write that book? I should be given immediate access to the documents, I should

be under the special protection of the Greek Government, I should have, as a matter of course, the entrée
to every circle of Greek Society which I might desire
to investigate, from the Court downwards. And all
my expenses would be paid.

Would I go to Athens? Would I go to heaven? Just
imagine if *you* had just come down from Oxford, were
still at heart an undergraduate, and were suddenly
given the opportunity of embarking on an adventure
which gave every promise of situations as fantastic as
ever occurred to the peppery imagination of William
le Queux! For, naturally, one guessed that, in an
undertaking of this sort, there would be a certain
element of danger. The Balkan countries have never
been exactly a health resort for political adventurers,
and what should I be but a political adventurer,
delving into secrets of which, at the moment, I knew
nothing, in a distant and romantic capital which was
alive with intrigue?

Would I go to Athens? Without a moment's delay
I sat down and wrote a telegram, saying that if
necessary I would start to-morrow.

Let us get straight on to Greece, for it is eas.er to
do that in a book than in the so-called *train-de-luxe*
which totters across Europe, falling over bridges,
blundering through ravines, and waiting for a whole
day at deadly looking hamlets in strange countries.
It is all right until you reach Fiume. Till then you
have a comfortable dining-car with regular meals,
and a sleeping compartment in which it is possible
to sleep and not to freeze. But after that, God help
you. They take off the dining-car, and you have to

depend for sustenance on what you have got with you. And if you have got nothing, it means that you have to clamber out of bed in the middle of the night and go into some filthy little railway café, to bargain for black olives and dusty chocolate and sour bread. At least, that was how things were in the winter of 1921.

A word about Belgrade, the capital of Yugo-Slavia, because it is, of all the cities I have ever seen, the most sinister and the most melancholy. It would appeal to Poe. We arrived at about dawn, and I woke up to look out on a dreary, broken-down station, snow-bound, and to hear the monotonous echo of some soldiers singing round a little fire which they had built on the platform to keep them warm. I dressed and went outside with some Greeks, who spoke bad French. We were all terribly hungry and were determined to eat some breakfast or die in the attempt.

What a sight when we stepped outside the station. You must imagine a background of leaden skies, and long, almost empty streets along which an occasional bullock cart silently plodded. In the foreground, however, all was colour and noise and animation, for it was market day, and the peasants from the outlying districts had all come in to sell their cattle. Never can there have been such a picturesque crew of rascals – rather like a chorus in the Chauve-Souris. The men with black beards, and stockings brightly worked in blue and crimson wools, the women with green aprons and yellow jackets, and odd-looking belts that seemed to be made of dyed leather. And they were all stamping about in the snow, shouting out in that dark, stinging language which sounds like Russian spoken by a devil. At least three fights were in progress, and the way they treated their animals made me feel that, unless I went straight into Belgrade, there would be a fourth.

We pushed our way through this unsavoury collection, and walked down the silent, desolate street in a sort of dream. There were no motors (I did not see a single motor in the whole of Belgrade) and very few horse-carriages. Almost every man we met was a soldier. And such soldiers! Dreary, pale, half-starved-looking creatures, slouching along like tramps, with uniforms that hung about them in rags and boots that had long been unfit for any human beings. Then, suddenly, we saw three officers, swaggering down towards us. A greater contrast it would be impossible to imagine. They were not only smart, they were superb. They glittered and shone and sparkled, they strutted, and puffed, and posed. They were the complete musical-comedy officer of the Balkans, their uniforms a dream of delight. And as they passed, a group of ragged soldiers sprang to attention, and remained stiff as corpses for fully a minute after the said officers had gone by. Discipline, what crimes are committed in thy name!

And then the breakfast! It was quite as depressing as a Dostoievsky novel. We had it at the best hotel in the place, and it consisted of bitter coffee, white butter made with goats' milk, and bread so sour that it was almost impossible to eat. There were no eggs, no meat, no sugar. One was back in war-time England again, *with* a difference.

Only one word more about Belgrade, and that must be to record the impression of amazement I had that this terrible hole of a place was the capital of one of the largest countries in Europe, of the country which, according to the economists, is going to be one of the most prosperous in the whole world. Make no doubt about it, Yugo-Slavia is a coming country. But if you could see its capital, the town which, by the august dispensation of the Peace-Makers, has been set in authority over many fair and cultured cities of the Austria that was, you would say it was a back slum of London, set on a hill, subjected to an earth-quake, and then cursed by the Creator.

They don't build houses to last in Belgrade, because they know that in ten years or so there will be another war, and the whole thing will be blown to pieces again. That is the sort of spirit one met the whole time. Nothing permanent. No trust. No faith. No hope. I looked into a photographer's shop and saw a photograph of the Parliament in session. So pompous, so threadbare, so utterly, damnably sad.

All this may have been the effect of a bad breakfast and a cold morning. But I think that you will admit that it is borne out by the facts.

Let us hurry to Greece. The next scene in the journey was when, at dawn, the train, with a last despairing effort, arrived at the frontier town of Ghev-Gelli, and stopped, panting. And this was Greece! This land of crystal sunlight, with the brown mountains against skies of burning blue. Greece! I felt like Linnæus, who went down on his knees at the first sight of English gorse; or like Cortez, when his eagle eye first gazed upon the Pacific, through the medium of Keats' Sonnet. Or like a great many other popular people who may all be found in *The Children's Encyclopædia*.

I dressed quickly, and went into a little restaurant that lay just behind the station. A brown-eyed maiden bustled forward and showed me to one of the four small tables. There was a spotless cloth on the table, and a big earthen bowl of violets. And for breakfast there was a huge glass of fresh milk, a chunk of coarse bread, and the sweetest honey that even Greek bees can ever have distilled. One felt that on such a diet, and under such sunshine, anybody could write masterpieces.

I had just swallowed my last spoonful of honey, and lit a cigarette, when there was a sound of tramping feet outside, a shouted word of command, a moment's silence, and then a babble of conversation. Soldiers! Greek soldiers! These must be inspected at once. I went to the door and saw, lined up, a small platoon of soldiers, clad in khaki, standing at ease. They were burnt almost black with the sunlight, were of rather under average height and were talking in a fierce and indigestible language. But what most attracted the eye was the superb young officer who was engaged in conversation with the conductor of the wagon-lit. He was the first (and almost the last) Greek I ever saw who gave one the impression of a statue come to life. And how smart he was! How his sword glistened in the sunlight, how his leather shone and his buttons sparkled!

Suddenly he turned, pointed in my direction, and started walking towards me. I hurriedly adjusted my tie, and wished that I had shaved. It didn't seem

to make much difference, but it made one feel somehow undressed. However, there was little time for
regret. The officer was already by my side.

'Monsieur Nichols?'

'Oui.'

He saluted, turned, and shouted to the soldiers.
They ceased talking. Shouting again. They sprang
to attention. Shouted again. They sloped arms.

This was terrifying. I also endeavoured to put a few
inches on my height, and frowned severely, which is
reputed to have an effect of making one look older.

'I come from the Military Commander of Mace-
donia,' he informed me. 'You are to be under his
special protection.'

'Thank you,' I said, in as deep and resonant a voice
as possible. 'It is very gracious of him.'

'I have also,' he remarked, 'to present you these
documents.' He handed me some papers decorated
with heavy seals. I took them, glanced at them, and
placed them inside my pocket.

'You will have no difficulty,' added this excellent
young man, 'in such things as customs. Athens has
been informed of your arrival. Everything will be
done to ensure your comfort.'

'I am more than honoured,' I said. I felt an awful
fraud, and was thankful that the Military Commander
himself was not present. If only one could have
grown a beard, or have developed pouches under the
eyes, or a cynical smile or *something* which would have
concealed the fact that one was really only an undergraduate, and not the distinguished author that they
were expecting. How marvellously Hall Caine would
have suited an occasion like this. He would probably

have emerged in a black coat, looking like a minor prophet, and have made some profound remark on the liberty of Greece. All I could do was to ask the young man to stand his soldiers at ease, which seemed an excellent suggestion and was promptly carried out.

We talked for a little longer, and then, in order to end a situation which was rapidly becoming unbearable, I informed him that I had business in the train which must be attended to. He sprang to attention, we shook hands, the soldiers clicked, sloped arms, right turned and stamped rhythmically out of the station. The last thing I saw was the glint of their rifles in the sun.

After waiting nearly the whole day at Ghev-Gelli, the train puffed out into the open country towards Athens at about five o'clock. I looked out on to the mountains and flower-filled valleys, dreaming in the late afternoon sunlight. The adventure had really begun.

And now, Athens.

We arrived at about seven o'clock in the evening, and all the things which my admirable and decorative soldier had foretold, came to pass. Various imposing people met me, my luggage slipped through the customs unopened, and I found myself outside the station while the other wretched people were still wrestling with officials.

Now, I am all for dramatizing the various episodes in one's life in order to get the utmost emotion from them. This seemed to be an episode well worthy of such treatment. And so, for this night, I planned to drive through the streets to my hotel in an open cab, have a jolly good dinner, and then go up to the Acropolis by moonlight alone.

I achieved all these delectable things. By various subterfuges I managed to get rid of the people round about, and found myself in the desired open cab driving slowly towards the main streets.

The streets of Athens at night! Take, as a model, Paris, and set it in surroundings of incredible beauty, hills that soar proudly above, a sea that stretches below, lit with the lights of a thousand ships. Fill it with dark, swarthy people, with eyes like stars, who do not so much walk as sway. Plant along its streets rows of pepper trees, whose feathery branches dance beneath the lamp-light. Sprinkle among the crowd young giants in the most picturesque uniform of Europe — a white kilt that makes them look, in the distance, like ballet girls. Build your houses of white marble, scatter their gardens with flowers, breathe over it all a spirit of gaiety and love, light it with a moon so clear and clean that it might be carved from the marble of the Acropolis — and then, perhaps, you will have a faint idea of Athens. Unless, from sheer incapacity, I have inadvertently been describing a Lyceum pantomime.

And then, most important of all, one could dine like a king in this paradise, and still can, for less than half a crown. The drachma was not nearly as low then as it is now, but this was what my dinner cost:

Wine 15 cents: A bottle of white wine — tasting of the tiny yellow grapes that are good enough to grow on the slopes of Mount Parnassus.

Omelette 12 *cents:* Superb. Greek hens are worthy of special praise.

Pilafe de Volaille A pilafe that brings to the dinner, 15 *cents:* as the cigarette advertisements say, something of the 'romance of the East.' Made *à la* Constantinople, its rice flavoured with essences which none but a Turk could contrive.

Yaorti 10 *cents:* It hailed originally from Bulgaria. It is a perversely succulent dish of sour cream and fresh cream mixed, iced, and sprinkled with sugar.

Savoury Apollo Born of an unholy but delectable 12 *cents:* union between the lobster and the crab, and baptized with a sauce of the cook's own invention.

Turkish Coffee Again the Eastern element. Con-5 *cents:* stantinople is close, you see – too close for the comfort of Greece. But, at least, it has taught them how to make coffee.

Grand Total, including wine, 69 cents.

And that is in the best hotel in Athens. If you go to any of the other restaurants, you will dine equally well for a good deal less.

But I want to take you with me up to the Acropolis, before we part company on this most thrilling of all nights. For the Acropolis is the personification of all Greece, it is the Crown of Athens, the eternal symbol raised aloft which proclaims that Greece has no kith nor kin with the crowded barbarians to the North, or the massed savages to the East. Oh! I know perfectly well that the Turk is a fine fellow – a finer fellow than the average Greek, and that probably modern Greece has little in common with the Greece that first lit the lamp of civilization in Europe. But Turkey has no Acropolis. And as long as those matchless columns hover, like a benediction over Athens, Greece will be *different* from her neighbours.

It was the night of the full moon. As we rattled up the narrow streets, the roads grew bumpier and bumpier, the lights more and more dim. A wonderful place, one thought at each street corner, for a murder. It would be dreadful to be murdered before seeing the Acropolis. After seeing it, nothing would matter. That at least was how I thought, as the cab swung round the final bend in the hill, drawing up beneath the clustered buildings, dreaming on their narrow cleft of rock.

How can I describe it, this milk-white miracle of beauty? Its beauty does not come from its antiquity alone, for here, among the columns of dim silver, stained with shadows of violet, one is away from Time. The temples soar to the stars, like white flowers eternally born anew. The same moon that lit the face of Alcibiades falls on each fragment of glittering marble, gilding the stone arms of its warriors and the silent faces of its maidens, and only yesterday it seems that the voice of Socrates must have echoed here, carried by this breeze through the cool, cleft spaces.

At night-time even modern Athens seems to fit into the dream without disturbing it. One stands by some broken, lovely fragment, looking over the hills on to the sparkling city beneath. It is a box of jewels spilt as an offering to the gods. The streets are strung into darkness like glimmering necklaces, and from far below comes the muffled whir and murmur of modern life. And then one shuts one's eyes again, and there is silence — the silence of eternal things . . .

I offer no apology for this sentimental outburst. I have no sympathy with the man who does not grow sentimental among the columns of the Acropolis. I have read about him in Freud, and he is a very dirty dog.

CHAPTER ELEVEN

Concerning the Confidences of a Queen

Oɴ the next day I was summoned to the Queen. I must here admit, with due shame and contrition, that I had never been to see a Queen before. I really don't know why. Still, the fact remains that I knew nothing whatever about Queens, especially Balkan ones. I had read about them in certain lurid accounts of themselves, from which I gathered that they must all be very temperamental, and I had seen photographs in the illustrated papers, from which I concluded that all photographers were Republicans. Beyond that, my mind was a blank.

Still, two things one knew instinctively about Queens. They liked to be called Ma'am, and they had to be approached in a morning coat. The ma'am business struck me as faintly ridiculous. I practised it while dressing, and pranced round the sunlight-flooded room saying, 'Yes ma'am, no ma'am, three bags full.' However, when one has on one's morning coat the ma'am becomes something rather awe-inspiring.

I had to be at the palace at eleven, and at fifteen minutes before that hour I entered a rickety 'amaxa,' drawn by two horses, and trundled over the bumpy streets towards my destination. A blue, blue sky above and all the houses glistening white. A faint breeze that drifted in from the sea. In the distance the Acropolis could be seen gleaming, like a white rose on a hill. Athens was bustling and wide awake. Little flower stalls made bright splashes of colour under the pepper trees. Outside on the boulevards people were drinking coffee and smoking cigarettes.

Now and then a lordly car would sweep by, and one would catch a glimpse of a rich merchant and his lady, the latter with pale face and crimson lips, and the glitter of diamonds that come from the Rue de la Paix. A little bit of Paris, a little bit of the East, a little bit of the classic past — that is Athens.

We swept through some wide gates after a certain controversy with two fierce sentries in white kilts. Charming people those sentries. I have always wanted to have one for a servant. They would create such a sensation in London. They have a scarlet turban, with a long tassel that hangs over the left shoulder, a tight-fitting blue jacket with rows of buttons like a page, a white sort of ballet skirt, shorter and more frilled than a kilt, long white stockings, and red shoes with huge black woollen rosettes on the toes. They told me that the costume was very comfortable, except for the shoes, which were always coming off.

I don't suppose we should ever have got past the gates had it not been for the kindly offices of the Royal Chamberlain, who was waiting for me, and took me straight to a reception room, then to another reception room, then to a third such, and finally left me to wait. I had not long to wait, for after about five minues an aide-de-camp appeared and told me that Her Majesty was ready to see me.

I followed him, noting the universal blue in which the palace was decorated. Blue curtains veiled the glare of the sunlight outside, casting a sort of haze into the quiet corridors. There were blue vases, and blue sweet-scented flowers, and an immense staircase covered with a blue carpet that was like a summer sky.

I negotiated the staircase successfully, walked down a few more miles of corridor, and was eventually ushered into a long room, very like an English drawing-room, in which Queen Sophie was standing.

I shall never forget my first sight of her, for she had the saddest face of any woman I have ever seen. Standing there, dressed entirely in black, a bowl of lilies by her side, her face rose from the shadows like one who has known every suffering. Beautiful? I am not sure about that. A beautiful expression, certainly. A beautiful bearing, too. But my first impression remains, also my last. The very air which she breathed seemed heavy with sadness.

(I don't wish to convey the impression that she was a sort of mute, a funereal figure. There were many days on which I saw her afterwards, in which she was one of the gayest and most sparkling of creatures. But the underlying note of tragedy would always recur.)

Her first words were anything but tragic.

'I'm so glad,' she said, 'that you don't try to kiss my hand. Some Englishmen seem to think that they must do it, and they always look so embarrassed.'

'Ought I to have done it — ma'am?' I said, wondering if I had let fall the first brick.

She spoke perfect English — or, rather, the sort of English that you and I speak, which is probably very far from perfect, but at least could not be accused of any foreign flavour.

114

'And now,' she said, 'before I tell you about Greece, for Heaven's sake tell me something about England. I haven't been there since the war, and' – here she shrugged her shoulders – 'I don't suppose I shall ever be able to go there again.'

I told her as much as I could. She was absolutely ravenous for information. Did they still plant the tulips in Hyde Park? Was the grass as green as ever in Kensington Gardens? (Oh, the green grass of England!) Were people giving many parties now? And what were the parties like, gay or sad? Had people got over the war at all? Were there any very pretty girls running about? Had I any idea whom the Prince of Wales was going to marry?

I gradually realized, as I endeavoured to supply some form of answer to this bewildering torrent of interrogatives, that here was a woman who was sick at heart for the country in which she had played as a child. For, after all, Kaiser's sister or no Kaiser's sister, Queen Sophie, when a girl, was brought up by her grandmother, Queen Victoria. She had Kensington Palace for her playground and her first paddling was performed on the beach at Eastbourne. And now, to be exiled, through no fault of her own, from the country which she loved so well, to be forbidden to see her friends, her relatives. . . .

'I suppose you have heard a great many stories about me?' she said, when I had exhausted England as a topic of conversation.

I nodded.

'For example?' she asked with a smile.

'That's not fair,' I said. It was quite impossible to

tell her even a fraction of the things one had heard.

'No. Perhaps it isn't. Well, I'll tell you a few of them. I was supposed, of course, to be in daily touch with my brother in Berlin, by wireless. I never quite gathered where the wireless was, but I believe they said it was in a tree in the garden. I was supposed to concoct elaborate plans for the destruction of the British Army. How, I don't quite know, because my husband always tells me I know nothing whatever about war. I was also reputed to teach all my children nothing but German. I presume that is why I have had nobody to teach them but an English governess who has been here for ten years, and whom you must meet. She's a very charming lady. In fact — I'm quite impossible. I wonder you dare come to see me.'

She laughed, and then became serious again.

'I want you to realize,' she said, 'something of the absolute — ' she paused for a word, her hands tightly clenched together — 'the absolute *agony* of my position at the beginning of the war. I loved England. I was brought up there. I had dozens of English relatives. I loved Germany, too. My brother was the Emperor. That sounds, I suppose, a crime, to love Germany. But try to clear your mind of the prejudice of the war. Try to realize — as I think we can now — that every German wasn't necessarily a devil, and that every Frenchman wasn't necessarily an angel. And then you will realize something of what I have suffered.'

She paused, and then said a sentence which I shall never forget. '*I was in a horrible No-Man's-Land of distraction!*

116

'What did I do? What *was* there to do, except to shut my eyes, and to think only of Greece? If I was to follow the struggle — first from this side and then from that — I should have gone mad. And so, as I say, I devoted myself to Greece. I nursed. I did my best in the hospitals. I busied myself in the gardens. I did anything but think . . .'

She rose to her feet with a sigh. 'Let's go into the garden, and forget all about it.'

She led the way from the room, and I followed her down endless corridors, in which sentries sprung to attention as we passed, and ladies-in-waiting smiled and curtsied from the shadows. Out in the sunshine we paused, and she looked at me with a curious smile.

'Before we go any farther,' she said, 'I want to show you something which will interest you. You have come out here to write a book, haven't you? Well — this thing which I shall show you, will make you, at least, *think*.'

We turned to the left, skirted the front of the palace, went through a sort of shrubbery, and then stopped.

'Look!' said the Queen.

I looked. Standing straight in front of me, against the wall, was a fourteen-inch shell. Not a pleasant-looking object. It was about the height of a child of six, and was, I should imagine, sufficiently powerful to blow up half the palace if it had landed in the right place.

'That shell,' she said quietly, 'was a present from the French. Every Englishman who sees it says that surely the French would not bombard a neutral

117

country? Surely the French, the apostles of culture, would not bombard, of all places in the world, Athens, the birthplace of culture? But you have a lot to learn. The date was December 2, 1916. Greece was still neutral. The bombardment began at ten o'clock in the morning, and went on intermittently till six at night.'

'And where were you all that time?'

She laughed. 'In the cellars. I can laugh at it now, but at the time it was not a laughing matter. You see, my children were with me. They were terrified. And I was distracted. Look at that shell, for example. If it had fallen three feet farther to the right, it would have gone straight through the window of my husband's study. He was in there at the time. It would not have been a very pleasant thing for the Allies, would it, to have had the murder of the King of a neutral country on their hands?'

There was nothing that I could say. I muttered something about looking into the matter.

'Yes. Look into it. That is all we ask of you, that you should try to find out the truth. And don't forget that though I may be the sister of the Kaiser, I'm also the daughter of the Princess Royal.'

I was nearly six months in Athens, with every possible facility for studying the truth, and I doubt even now if I discovered it. That the Queen was utterly sincere and genuine, I do not doubt. That the French, in the desperation of the struggle, behaved foolishly, I am convinced. But as to the exact measure of blame, I remain undecided.

However, I did not set out to write a book of political arguments, but a book of human studies. And I hope that by this tiny sketch a few people at least will see Queen Sophie in a more kindly light than has hitherto been thrown upon her.

CHAPTER TWELVE

Strange Tales of a Monarch and a Novelist

A FORTNIGHT later I was sitting in the lounge of the Hotel Grande Bretagne, when a message arrived saying that Tino would like to see me at six o'clock.

It was then a little after four, and the hectic, unnatural pageant of Athenian Society was drifting by in full swing. Look well at that pageant, for Athens, in this January of 1922, seemed a sinking city in a doomed land, and there is a romance about such cities which is denied to the more prosperous metropoles of the West, a romance which comes from the knowledge that everybody is playing a part, and that a hundred undercurrents of intrigue are running between the apparently smooth surface of the waters.

There are several beautiful people in the lounge, and the most attractive of all are Russians. There are, at the time, nearly ten thousand Russian refugees in Athens, and their plight is such that, thinking of them, it is not too easy to sleep at nights. The women by now have mostly found 'protectors,' accepting with a bored smile a situation which, five years ago, they would have found impossible. Some have attached themselves to rich merchants of the Levant, others have wormed their way into the affections of the military, a few have even achieved the success of an unhappy marriage. And now they are all sitting in this lounge, smoking cigarettes, and blowing out the smoke through purple and impassive lips, waiting.

The men are worse off than the women. Look at

this one who approaches me. He was once an officer in the Imperial Guard. To-day he wears a patched white coat, well tied in at the waist, and blue trousers of a common Russian soldier. One thin white hand is grasping a stick, and in the other is a little tray containing his paintings — such pathetic, amateurish paintings, which he is trying to sell. He stands in front of me and tries to smile. It is a grotesque caricature of a smile — a little twitch of the lip. His whole body is trembling as though from a violent chill. Shell shock, and one lung already destroyed.

I buy one of his little paintings, and try to look as though I were buying it because I wanted it. He is of the stuff which gentlemen are made of. If there had been no war, he would have been a smart young fellow playing gentle havoc with hearts in Petrograd.

He passes on, and is lost in the crowd of cosmopolitan adventurers. There is a fat man from Paris, who is reputed to be doing a big deal in raisins, and looks as though he had eaten most of them in a fit of absent-mindedness. There is a little row of very silly *soignée* Greek women, eyeing each other's dresses, and pining for Paris. They think it chic to talk French, and to affect to despise this backward, out-of-the-way place that they call Athens. There are several young officers on leave from the front. They stare moodily in front of them, for they, at least, have a tale to tell, having been mobilized, some of them, for seven years, and having seen the army gradually losing its rifles, its boots, and its morale. There are several prosperous-looking Germans, gabbling at the tops of their voices. One of them has a row of enormous volumes on Greek statuary in front of him.

I pay for my tea with a bank-note cut in half – a strange procedure worthy of explanation. Greece was in the direst financial straits. It was quite useless to suggest a new loan, for nobody would subscribe to it. And so an ingenious chancellor suddenly thought of a way by which the peasants could all be made to disgorge half of their savings. Every paper note in the kingdom had to be cut in half. The left half must be immediately given to the bank, where it would be credited to one's account, with an interest of 5 per cent. The right half might be used as currency. Thus, a note worth a pound automatically became worth ten shillings cash, the other ten shillings being placed in the bank. All this cutting and snipping of notes had to be done in a fortnight.

I arrived at the palace at six o'clock, and was shown up to Tino's study – a pleasant, English-looking room, with plenty of books, and windows that gave on to one of the prettiest parts of the garden. He was sitting down on the sofa, reading, and as he rose to greet me he seemed enormous. He must have been at least six feet six, and six feet six in a soldier who holds himself well erect is a good deal more than many of the drooping six foot sixers one sees slouching down Piccadilly.

It was characteristic of him, as I afterwards learnt, that as soon as we had shaken hands he almost pushed me into a chair, practically stuffed a cigar between my lips (I loathe cigars) and before I had time to light it, plunged straight into the heart of the controversy which was raging round his throne.

'You realize,' he said, 'that you're talking to a King who's disowned by the greater part of Europe, and also by the United States. Don't you?'

I did realize it.

'Very well, then. We are therefore in a position to talk quite frankly. I've certainly nothing to lose by telling you the truth.' He paused. 'However shocking it may be,' he added with a grim smile, 'I'm under no sort of illusion as to how they regard me in England. I've seen caricatures of myself in every conceivable attitude in the English papers — some of them rather funny as a matter of fact, funnier, at any rate, than the German ones. Perhaps it never struck you that they'd caricature me in German papers? I assure you they do. You see, Germany doesn't like me any more than England. I am altogether a most unpopular person. Except in Greece.' Again the grim smile.

'However, we didn't come here to talk about caricatures. I just want to give you a few ideas, that's all. You can verify them afterwards at your leisure. The first thing on which I want you to fix your attention is the beginning of the war. When war was declared I received a telegram from the Kaiser. He writes admirable telegrams, my brother-in-law. It suggested that I should at once throw in my lot with the Central Powers. I was at Tatoy when the telegram arrived, having a very innocent but a very excellent tea. As soon as I had read it I remember saying to my wife "Good God! He seems to forget that Greece is practically an island." By which, I was referring, you see, to the consummate foolishness of the Kaiser in thinking that any Greek in his right mind — whatever his private sentiments – should consider, even for a moment, declaring war against the rulers of the seas.

'I then summoned certain ministers, and drafted my reply. If you take the trouble to look it up you will see that it was an emphatic refusal. I tried to make it polite, but apparently the Kaiser didn't think it was polite enough. In any case, he was particularly rude to my minister in Berlin, Monsieur Theotokis.

'Nobody has ever quoted that telegram. They probably never will, because it doesn't fit in with the Tino legend. However, it is there, in all the blue books. Just have a look at it when you get the time.

'The next thing I want you to consider is my various offers of help to the Allies. I shan't particularize because you can find them all in the official résumés of diplomatic correspondence which every country publishes. Besides, dates and things of that sort are dull.

'What was my position at the beginning of the war? What was, rather, the position of Greece? I will tell you. We were in a pretty bad way. We had none too much money. We had been exhausted by a long series of wars. We needed, above all things, rest. However, when the Great War broke out, there were two courses open to us. We could either remain neutral or we could join the Allies. The idea of throwing our lot in with Germany was absolutely out of the question, for, as I have said before, Greece is to all intents and purposes, an island, and it would have been suicidal to fight England, even had any of us wanted to do so.

'Well, as you will see in the blue books, I offered my assistance. It was refused. Why? Because, according to Lord Grey, it was important not to *froisser* Bulgaria, not to annoy King Ferdinand!' He brought his fist down on the table with a bang which quite shattered my cigar ash.

'I warned Grey,' he said. 'I warned your Foreign Office, not once but half a dozen times, that Bulgaria was arming against you, that she was not to be trusted, that she was about to throw in her lot with Germany. I was not heeded. I was either answered with polite shrugs of diplomatic shoulders, or I was not answered at all.'

He stared in front of him gloomily, and when he resumed it was in a quieter voice.

'You know the next stage. The Dardanelles. Now every third-rate politician and every third-rate staff officer in the countries, not only of the Allies but of the Central Powers, has very decided opinions upon the Dardanelles. They say, "If only Tino had done this," or "If only Tino had done that," or "If only the Turks had been a few days later, or the Allies a few days sooner," or "If only Winston had had his way." In fact they go on saying "if only" until the whole thing becomes a tragic farce.

'But I tell you, young man, that I *know* the Dardanelles. I *know* the Black Sea. I *know* that there are certain ways in which Constantinople can be attacked, and certain ways in which it can't. I know a good deal more about both the military and the naval sides of the question than even your friend Mr. Winston Churchill, and my staff probably know more than I do myself. Don't you see that for generations the eyes of Greece have been fixed on Constantinople? Don't you realize that in the heart of every Greek there lies the dream that one day he will be able to throw his cap into the air at the news that Greece has re-entered into the inheritance which every Greek regards as his natural birthright? Why, there is even a legend that when there sits on the Greek throne a monarch of the name of Constantine and a Queen of the name of Sophie, ... Greece will capture Constantinople. A foolish legend, perhaps you may say. But the conditions of it were fulfilled when, thirty years ago, I married my wife. And the coincidence has been working in my people's imagination ever since.'

He paused, rose from his seat, and went over to the window. And when he went on talking it was with his eyes fixed on the quiet lawns outside.

'Now,' he resumed, 'I'm not saying that this dream is right or wrong. I'm merely telling you that the dream is there. And since it is there, and since the Greeks, though they may be superstitious, are also a practical people, it stands to reason, doesn't it, that the Greek Officers and Staff, not only of the army but of the navy, should have the whole situation at their finger-ends? Doesn't it? Tell me. Am I being logical or am I not?'

I reassured him on that point.

Very well then,' he continued. 'When I first heard of the Dardanelles Campaign, I knew that it was doomed to failure. I knew it in my very bones. I expressed my opinion in public and in private. I was called a pro-German because I would not join it, because I would not send at least 10,000 Greek soldiers to help the Allies. Was I right or wrong? I knew that if I sent 10,000 soldiers there would be 10,000 widows in Greece in a few weeks. And I was damned if I would do it.'

And then he said something which made me sit up.

'*If I had been pro-German I could have wrecked the whole Allied course in the Near East as easily as I can flick my fingers.*' And he flicked his fingers in my face.

'How?'

He laughed. 'You're an inquisitive youth, aren't you? Well, I'll explain.'

'You may remember,' he said, 'that in the autumn of 1915 the Allies were in a very bad way. The armies of Austria and Germany were sweeping down through the Balkans like a great black cloud. Serbia was overrun and desolated. The whole of the north was in the grip of the Central Powers. Bulgaria was closing in on the east. The only refuge was – Greece.

'I had already violated my neutrality in favour of the Allies by allowing General Sarrail, the Allied Commander, to use Salonika as a base for his troops. A fat lot of thanks I got for it – but that is by the way. I was therefore in an exceedingly difficult position. If I allowed the Allies to retreat over my frontier I could hardly, as a neutral monarch, forbid the Germans from doing the same thing. To do so would be tantamount to a declaration of war against Germany.

'Consider the position if you want to prove that I was *not* pro-German. Here was the Allied Army retreating into Greece, beaten and exhausted. They were cut off from the north and from the east. My own army was in their rear, fresh and intact. *If I had wished to declare War on the Allies could you possibly imagine a more favourable opportunity?* I could have wiped out Sarrail without the loss of more than a thousand men. The whole of the Balkans would have been completely, irrecoverably German. And the war would not have ended as it has done.

'But what did I do? For that I would again refer you, not to the newspapers, but to the official documents. I sent a telegram to the Kaiser stating that if one German soldier advanced a yard over the Greek frontier, I should consider it a hostile act, and should declare war. In other words, I saved the Allies at one of the most critical moments of the struggle.'

He stopped abruptly. 'And that,' he said, 'is all I've got to say to you this evening.'

I rose to go, feeling a little bewildered. When I returned to my hotel I wrote down the whole of the foregoing conversation, word for word, and I think it is almost verbally accurate.

And that is all I am going to write about the Greek question, for I have discovered, on bitter experience, that people don't care a damn about it, and that the whole question bristles with difficulties. I only write to ease my own conscience, and to pay a humble little tribute to two people whom I learnt to regard as friends.

One cannot, however, write about Tino without also writing about Compton Mackenzie. It may seen a long step from the most hated monarch of Europe to a man who used to be one of England's most popular novelists, but it is not quite so long as you might imagine, for, according to Greek Royalists,

Compton Mackenzie was the evil genius of Greece during the war.

In early 1915 (I think it was) he was appointed head of the Anglo-French police in Athens. A curious appointment, one would think, but those days of chaos abounded in curious appointments, and at least one could say about Compton Mackenzie, that he had a sense of style. They told me that he fell out of a balloon somewhere in the Near East, and was on the point of being invalided out of the army when this appointment suddenly became vacant. He accepted it with alacrity, for he had very clear ideas on the Greek question. The first of these ideas was that Tino was violently pro-German and as treacherous as they make them. The second was that he himself was called, whatever the sacrifice, to lead a crusade of neo-Hellenism against the Turk, the Bulgarian, the German, or any other nation that got in the way.

His methods of work, they alleged, were remarkable. He is said to have taken a little office, and there concocted his wicked schemes, clad in garments more fitted for the less reputable colleges of Oxford than for His Majesty's Service. I was told of purple waistcoats, long black walking-sticks, heavy cloaks lined with green silk, black stock ties. It cannot be true, but at least there is something most intriguing in the picture of this young and rather decorative relic of the nineties carrying out Balkan intrigues against a background of classic pillars and traitorous monarchs.

They alleged also (I am scattering that blessed word 'alleged' all over the place, as a sort of disinfectant against libel actions) – they alleged that on several occasions he tried to murder King Constantine – rather hot work for the head of the British police stationed in a neutral and officially friendly country. I saw a newspaper cutting of some Greek paper in which there was a photograph of one of the King's bodyguard, together with a long legend that Compton Mackenzie had bribed him to put poison in the King's wine. The story ran something like this. Mackenzie, having found out that bombs were too dangerous and that daggers made too much mess, decided that he would employ the more cleanly and efficient aid of arsenic. He obtained the arsenic and also managed, somehow or other, to get hold of a very simple and child-like soldier who was in attendance on the King, at a time when the King's health was giving rise to grave anxiety.

'Do you know why the King is so ill?' he is alleged to have said to the Evson.

'No?'

'Because he is bewitched by the Queen.'

Here the Evson began to take keen interest. He knew all about witcheries, and such-like.

'Yes.' Mackenzie is alleged to have continued. 'And the only way in which we can break the spell is for you to put this powder into his glass when he is at dinner. It is a very wonderful powder – the crushed essence of a herb that only grows in England. When he has drunk it you will find that immediately he will be cured.'

After a little persuasion, the story runs, and a rather larger amount of bribery, the Evson departed with the arsenic, promising faithfully that he would give it

130

to the King. But as the evening shadows fell his courage failed him. Supposing that, after all, the herb should not do its work? Supposing that it did his master actual harm? No. It was really a little risky. And so he went to a certain Court official and told him the story. Consternation. Curses against England. Salvation of King Constantine. Tableau.

A childish story of course. But it was believed by a great many otherwise sane people. And it only shows you how careful you must be in the Secret Service.

Another, and even more lurid tale, was told about Mr. Compton Mackenzie. I never saw any newspaper cuttings on the subject, because I don't think it got into the Press. But I *was* furnished with a great many strange-looking documents, much thumbed, and decorated at all the available corners with red sealing-wax. This story was also concerned with an alleged attempt by the English novelist on King Constantine's life – an attempt that, if it had been true, would have been about the most ingenious piece of inventive work that he had ever done.

In the summer of 1915 (I think that is the right date), the King's Palace at Tatoy – some twenty miles outside Athens – was burnt. For miles round the heath and scrub were devastated by fire. The King was in his Palace at the time and only escaped by a miracle. And even so, several of his bodyguard were burned to death.

All this, the Royalists alleged, was the work of Compton Mackenzie. With devilish ingenuity he was described as having obtained the services of some half-dozen of the riff-raff of Athens, among whom was a German prostitute in the pay of the Allies, of having bought a quantity of petrol and benzine, hired four motor-cars, and set out from a low café at dawn in order to accomplish his dirty work. The plan was to surround the Palace with fire from all sides, so that there should be no possible escape, and with this object some six points had been marked on a map, in the form of a wide circle, which were to be soaked with benzine and set alight. The wind would do the rest.

I myself saw a map which was supposed to have been stolen from Compton Mackenzie's headquarters, but had, as a matter of fact, been manufactured by my informant. It showed a number of mysterious crosses, and subsequent inquiry proved that fires had actually broken out, almost simultaneously, at all these places, proving beyond a shadow of doubt that the 'accident' was not an accident at all. But why poor Compton Mackenzie should have been accused of it I could never quite make out.

CHAPTER THIRTEEN

From the Regal to the Ridiculous

THOSE little Balkan Courts were terribly pathetic. They always gave me the impression of a rather threadbare musical comedy on tour. There was so much pomp, such a glitter of uniforms, and so little money. I shall never forget my first sight of a Royal car. Tino was in it, plumed and feathered, and were it not for the large crown painted on the back, one would have said that the car was a dilapidated Ford. So dilapidated that the tyres were bound up with tape and seemed to be of different shapes. I watched the car trundle out of sight, and just as it turned the corner there was a loud bang. The first tyre had burst, and Tino had to get out and watch his chauffeur struggling in the dust.

If Queen Sophie had sold her pearls, which were amazingly beautiful, the whole Royal Family would have had plenty for the rest of their lives. But I suppose she could not do that, since they were Crown jewels. As things were, the severest economy had to be used to make both ends meet.

One day I went to tea with her and after tea we walked, as usual, in the garden. It was looking exquisite that evening, the bougainvillea, a mass of purple, dripping from the walls, and all the lemon trees heavy with golden fruit. By and by we came to a little pond of marble, which was empty.

'How lovely this must be when it is filled with water,' I said.

'Yes. But I don't know when we shall be able to fill it.'

'Is the drought as bad as all that?'

She shook her head. 'No. I wasn't referring to the drought. The pond has to be cleaned before it can be filled. And that means another gardener. And gardeners cost 15 drachmæ a day.'

Now fifteen drachmæ, at that period, was about half a crown. Can you imagine a Queen not being able to have a pond cleaned out because she had not the necessary half a crown?

And yet, during the war, people used to talk ridiculous nonsense about the Greek Royal Family revelling in gold owing to the marriage of the American millionairess, Mrs. Leeds, with Prince Christopher, the King's youngest brother. Sheer nonsense. She was not allowed to do so. I believe that she was very generous and sweet in giving presents in the ordinary run of affairs, but as for financing Tino's family (let alone financing Greece, as they said she did) – that was quite out of the question.

Princess Irene – one of the most attractive girls I have ever seen – once said to me, 'Isn't the price of clothes appalling?'

Mindful of tailor's bills, I fervently agreed with her.

'I want to get some new evening frocks,' she added, 'but I can't get any under twenty pounds.'

If only things had been different, what a paradise the Queen would have made of Athens, and of the Palace in particular. 'Before the war,' she said, 'we had all the plans ready. We were going to have a beautiful new hotel in Constitution Square, we were going to make the roads good again, we were going to plant thousands of trees all over the mountains. And I had dozens of English furniture catalogues which I used to read and read, thinking of all the lovely things we should have in the Palace. All that is finished — absolutely finished. We must get along as we can. I can't even afford to have the English magazines now. . . .'

And then, 'Isn't it perfectly *appalling* the way we always talk about money nowadays? I never used to. My mamma would have thought it terrible. But now it's, "I can't afford this, and I can't afford that." And it's such a dreary topic of conversation. Let's talk about something else.'

We both laughed, and talked instead, of England.

Endless comedies arose out of the fact that the Royal Family were not recognized by the Allies, because the members of the British Legation had to be officially unaware of their very existence. Francis Lindley, our Minister at Athens, said to me that it was damnably awkward for him, because sometimes he would meet Tino in the street, or driving in a motor-car, and they both had to look the other way.

A regular game of hide-and-seek sometimes ensued. I remember once going with Bridget Lindley and some others from the Legation to play tennis in the gardens of the British School of Archæology. We had a divine game of tennis, and when it was over strolled round the garden looking for flowers. We had just turned a corner when, there, a few yards in front of us was the Queen of Greece, with a lady-in-waiting. With a hoot of dismay the young ladies from the Legation turned on their heels and fled.

135

(It sounds rude, but it was the only thing they could have done.) I was left alone to greet the Queen.

'Who were those girls who rushed away like that?' said the Queen.

'Oh – they were just some people who have been playing tennis.'

'Yes. But who *were* they?'

I had to tell her that they were the Lindleys.

She made a little gurgling noise of laughter. 'I see. Isn't it ridiculous?' And then . . . 'We might be such good friends. It's a pity. . . .'

Occasionally, however, some man from the Legation, in an access of boldness, *would* visit the Palace, and a very good time he was given. But these things had to be worked out with great secrecy, because naturally, if the Minister knew, he would be forced to take severe measures against the offenders. There was one young man (I can't, of course, give his name) whom we smuggled into the Palace one afternoon, and the arrangements for getting him there and back were worthy of an *opéra bouffe* conspiracy. We had to go in a closed motor and be hustled up a back staircase into the boudoir of a lady-in-waiting. It was then arranged that the Queen and some of the Princesses should cross the garden, come up another staircase, and enter a few minutes later. We used to make absurd jokes about it, saying that the Queen might suddenly shoot down the chimney, or that the Englishman should disguise himself as a piano-tuner, and enter in that manner.

It was at one of these tea-parties that the Queen, becoming serious for a moment, gave us just a hint of some of the tortures she must have suffered in exile. 'When we were exiled from Greece,' she said, 'the only place which was open to us was Switzerland. We went there, and stayed at an hotel. I wanted to be just like the other guests – I wanted, as they said I was no longer a Queen, *not* to be a Queen, just to be an ordinary human being. Staying in the hotel were several of my old English friends, whom in days gone by I had known quite intimately. They used to be of my party in the opera; I have danced at their houses, dined with them. One and all, they cut me dead. I shouldn't have minded that – for, after all, there are *ways* of cutting people, aren't there? But they did it in the unkindest way possible, publicly – not only to myself but to my husband – leaving any room that I entered, and staring me straight in the face as they went out. Now – it isn't like English people to do that, is it? And yet they did. It was not till I picked up some of the English papers, and learnt what they were saying about us over there, that I realized the reason for it.'

None of the restrictions which so hampered any members of the Legation when they wanted to go to the Palace applied to me, because I had no official position, and nobody seemed to know what I was doing in Athens. But Athens is a very small place, and very soon some remarkable legends began to spread about me. Some people said I was in the pay of the Bolsheviks, others in the pay of Germany, others that I was a young English millionaire forced to fly my country because of some scandal connected with a Greek lady, and that I was in Athens to settle it up. Being very young, I rather enjoyed these legends and had Compton Mackenzie not apparently forestalled me, should probably have purchased a wardrobe in keeping with the part I was supposed to be playing, consisting of a red tie, a pair of check knickerbockers, and a heavy gold watch-chain. However, I contented myself with a black evening cloak, lined with pale grey satin, that called forth rude and Bacchic remarks from the ladies of light virtue who lurked under the lemon trees of an evening.

I only realized, however, the true thrill of being a political intriguer one night towards the end of my stay in Athens when I was walking home, along the deserted sea-front, after a night's gambling at a little roulette place near the harbour. It sounds very dissipated, and I suppose, in some ways, it was. Here is the story:

. The Greeks are born gamblers. They would gamble away their final drachma on the slightest provocation, and frequently do so. Every other day in the streets of Athens one sees boys going round with long slender sticks, on which are pinned fluttering tickets of blue and white – and very pretty they look, rustling in the wind. These are lottery tickets, and have a tremendous sale. I had often purchased them, without any result, and finding some sort of gambling essential to existence, decided to throw in my lot with the roulette players of the Piræus.

I wish you could have seen that Greek gambling house. It lay in a rather deserted position facing the sea, along a road that had never been finished. On a moonlight night you could see from its windows the white sails of the ships that search for sponges and tunny fish among the waters of the Archipelago, but on other nights you would see nothing at all except a solitary lamp-post outside the door.

Inside, one discovered a sordid room, containing one long table, round which were congregated a remarkable assemblage of persons. There were Russian ladies of apparent wealth, Italians, swarthy and silent, excitable Greek merchants, now and then a German, some odd-looking Americans, and Venizelists and Royalists all jumbled together, drinking quantities of bad whisky and smoking black cigarettes.

The value of a classical education, in such surroundings, was immediately apparent. For one thing, the numbers were almost exactly the same as one learnt at school, and sometimes even the pronunciation also. For example, ochto was eight and deka was ten. That was a great help. In addition, 'mavro,' for black, sounded like an old friend, and it was easy to recognize 'coichinou' the word cochineal (with which, if I remember rightly, the Greek ladies used to dye their robes in days gone by).

Play seemed to me to be very high that night, although, as my later and more abandoned years have taught me, it was not. Still, a man with heavy pouched eyelids and a made-up bow had a habit of putting fifty pounds on a single number, and sometimes winning it, which made my hundred drachma pieces look very foolish. However, I successfully lost twenty pounds, and feeling exceedingly irritable left the room.

It was then about two o'clock in the morning. I hadn't any money to pay for a taxi, and in any case there were no taxis about. And so I started on the walk home – about seven miles.

Now, the streets of Athens at night, especially of this part of Athens, are not as the streets of Piccadilly. For one thing, they are execrably lit. For another they contain large holes in the middle of the road, in which it would be quite possible to bury a dead horse. For another they contain dogs, lean, snarling, yellow-fanged dogs that rush out from the darkness, growling and yelping, and taking an unhealthy interest in one's heels.

Several such came out during my journey home. I put on a wooden expression, lifted my feet very high, took quick short steps, and muttered at intervals 'pretty doggy, pretty doggy.' It seemed the only thing to do. And by and by the pretty doggies departed, though the sound of their strident voices still echoed in the distance.

I was now on a long, straight road, bounded on either side by pepper trees and shrubberies of orange and lemon. Suddenly out of the shadows appeared a figure . . . the figure of a youngish man in a badly fitting black coat. It sounds dramatic and it *was* dramatic. Worse even than the dogs.

This person accosted me. Where was I going? (He spoke in French, and was, I believe, a Frenchman.)

I was going home, thank him very much.

So was he.

Indeed.

It was pleasant, was it not, to have company on such a lonely road?

Delightful. (Pretty doggy, pretty doggy.)

Especially on so warm a night.

Yes.

Ah! but I had not experienced the summer. That was epouvantable.

I looked at him quickly. How did he know that I had not 'experienced' the summer?

'I know you quite well,' he said. And he calmly gave my name, age, address, and occupation.

This was all very odd. I walked a little more quickly. Athens was still some five miles away. I could see the Acropolis gleaming like a distant rock of refuge. A nasty young man, I thought.

Then he began to talk. He talked like a gramophone running at three times its normal speed. A high unnatural voice. A superfluity of gesture. And all about King Constantine. How he had betrayed the Allies. How he had kept a private submarine. How he was a knave, a poltroon, a pig, a female dog. How he had a hoard of German gold. And how. . .

Here, at a bend in the road, he suddenly stopped, gripped my arm, looked me straight in the eyes and said:

'And you – you who call yourself an Englishman – are helping him!'

I regarded him as calmly as the circumstances warranted. And in English I said:

'You appear to be a little mad!'

'Mad?' He laughed hysterically, and then – (it sounds ridiculous, but it is perfectly true) – he drew from his pocket a revolver, and though not exactly levelling it at me, put it quite as close as was agreeable, and said:

'This will tell you to speak of madness.'

Which was highly disturbing. The sudden cessation of the gabble of chatter, the wild look on his face, the revolver. Something had to be done. I did it. I smiled, drew in my breath, and executed a powerful high kick. It hit him, by a miracle, on the wrist; the thing went off, spluttering up the gravel; he dropped it with a howl; I kicked it again on to the grass, and then I ran.

All very unheroic. But, on the whole, safe. I ran and I ran down that lonely road, and by the time I had finished running the first streaks of dawn were in the sky, and I was feeling acute pains in my side, my legs, my knees, my brain, everywhere. But at least one had the satisfaction of having outwitted (or outdistanced) a very nasty young man.

Nothing like that ever happened again. I received anonymous letters, all threatening things highly unpleasant. But whether they were from the young man in question I never discovered. And they never materialized.

My last night in Athens was spent at the Palace. The Queen had asked me to stay on a little longer in order to trot round with her nephew, Prince Philip of Hesse. I was very glad that I did so, for not only was he a most agreeable young man but by staying those few extra days I also met the Queen of Roumania, who had come hurriedly down to Athens in order to be with her daughter (the Crown Princess of Greece) who was seriously ill.

I shall never forget my first sight of the Queen of Roumania. We were all sitting down in the main salon – Tino, Queen Sophie, Princess Irene, the Crown Prince and Princess of Roumania, some other members of the Court, and myself. The door was slightly open, and through it one could see a long corridor, dimly lighted. I looked down the corridor and I saw coming towards us a figure in trailing robes of white, walking slowly, with head erect, like some divine Lady Macbeth. As she approached, and paused in the doorway, I thought that I had never seen a woman more lovely. The long white sleeves of silk, the girdle of silver at her waist, the hint of diamonds in her hair, the ropes of pearls round her neck. And the face – wide eyes, a forehead that was one hundred per cent. intelligence, a beautiful drooping mouth . . . it is rather useless to attempt to describe her. A photograph will do her less injustice than my pen.

Luckily, I was very soon able to have a long talk with her.

Here, clipped of its 'ma'ams' and 'majesties' is what we talked about:

MYSELF: Is it a fearful bore to be a Queen?

THE QUEEN: It depends what sort of a Queen you are.

MYSELF: But even a Queen like yourself? Don't you long sometimes to be able to get away from it all, to be terribly simple, to have all sorts of adventures which you can't have now?

THE QUEEN (nodding, a little sadly): There are moods, of course. But I like being a Queen because I glory in the fact that perhaps I am of some use.

Here she paused, and said, with a smile: 'You know, I understand a great deal more about life than you might believe. If I had been Marie Antoinette, *I* should never have asked why the people could not eat cake. And you must not think that because I am a Queen, my knowledge of life and "adventure," as you call it, is only gained from novels. Do you know one of my chief regrets? It is that I am not in a position to publish a novel which would deal with life from every aspect.

'I said "publish," not write. I could begin to write it to-morrow, if I wanted, but when it came out, everybody would say, "How can she know about things like this? How can a woman who sits half her life in her palace" (the last thing I ever do) "know about the ways, the intrigues, the marriages, the love-affairs, the sordid squabbles for money, that are part of our daily lives?" And saying that, they would reject my book in advance. But I *do* know,' (thumping her hand on the table), 'I *do* know. . . .'

'Then,' I asked her, 'do you manage to write at all? I mean, do you find any way of getting rid of what one might call creative emotion?'

'Oh yes. I write fairy stories. Nobody can accuse me, in those, of knowing more than I ought to do.' She laughed. 'Perhaps that does not quite express my meaning, but you understand, don't you? Fairy love, fairy honour, fairy intrigue, fairy magic – in those I express all the emotions which otherwise I should be forced to keep to myself. And Roumania is full of fairies! Really it is. Full to the brim. When I first came out there, from England, I hardly understood how deeply my people were versed in folk-lore, how passionately real the little elves and sprites were to every peasant on the hills. But I understand now,

and I, too, have caught something of that spirit.
'Do you know,' she added suddenly, 'that I have
written a fairy film? I wish you could see it. It's
rather fascinating. It has a method of production
which I think is rather new. Some parts of it have
been undeveloped, so that you get the impression
of a moving *negative*. That is to say, all the figures
have white hair, white eyes, white clothes, dark
hands and faces, and all sorts of queer and very
attractive shadows. If you can imagine those figures
made very small (which is quite possible) and then
imagine them dancing in a sort of half-silhouette
over the crest of a hill . . . can you?'

She had spoken with such animation, such intense
interest, that her face was quite transfigured.

A very remarkable woman, I thought, as she
drifted away to talk to somebody else. And largely
because, of all the Queens in Europe, she is the only
one who really dramatizes her position. She is, in
the best sense of the word, a *poseuse*, by which I mean
that she knows exactly how to present herself to the
public imagination. Realizing, as she does, that in
these days the Throne has to borrow a great deal of
thunder of the stage if it is to keep its position, and
that showmanship is half the craft of sovereignty,
she acts accordingly. All her gestures are studied
. . . sometimes daring, sometimes startlingly 'un-
conventional,' as her recent journalistic confessions
have amply shown.

But they remain the gestures of a Queen.

CHAPTER FOURTEEN

In which Sir William Orpen and Mrs. Elinor Glyn reveal
their Souls

AND now, on returning to London, I decided
that it was time to 'become a journalist.' So
many hundreds of otherwise sane young men have
made the same decision, without success, that it
really might be worth while to tell them just one
thing about it. They have such glorious dreams, at
Oxford, over a cigarette and a whisky and soda, of
writing palpitating articles for vast prices, that it is
only fair to disillusion them.

The one thing which the embryo journalist must
realize is that mere writing is only one-quarter of
his equipment. He may be able to produce brilliant
articles, to star every page with epigrams, to com-
pose perorations that wring the heart, to evolve
leaders that would stir the Empire, and still not be a
successful journalist.

He must certainly begin at the beginning. And to
do that he must have a hide of brass. Brass, I said.
No other substance is strong enough. He *must* ring
up irate Duchesses at midnight and ask them what
they think of bobbed hair. He must do it, at any
rate for a few months, for it is only right for him to
know how it feels. He *must* go to successful stock-
brokers and ask them what they think of the financial
situation. He *must* visit the Zoo and grovel about
in dirty cages to see if the latest lizard has laid an
egg, or if the latest elephant has recovered from its
pain. He must do it, even though it makes him feel
ill, even though he blushes over the telephone, is
terrified by elephants, and feels like hitting the

stockbroker fair and square on the chin. One day he will be telling other people to do these things. He cannot tell them unless he has done the things himself.

For — and this is the whole point of the matter — three-quarters of modern journalism consists in making other people say things, not in saying them yourself. Do not hope, my young friend, that anybody will pay any attention to *your* articles. You may get them accepted from time to time, but unless you are an overpowering genius you will not make much of a living out of it.

I could write a lot more on the subject but I won't. Nobody ever wants advice. It is enough to say that in the August of 1922 I 'got on' to a paper.

The first man I ever 'interviewed' was Sir William Orpen. Really, one could hardly call it an 'interview,' for it merely consisted in having tea with him, eating quantities of very excellent cucumber sandwiches, and smoking many cigarettes.

After about the tenth sandwich, I said, 'I have to interview you, and I haven't the vaguest idea how to begin.'

'Have another sandwich.'

'I shall be sick.'

'That's what they're for. I don't want to be interviewed.'

'But you said you would.'

'Did I? Well, fire away.' (Pause.) 'You're a dud sort of journalist aren't you? Where's your notebook? And your pencil that ought to leave indelible ink stains all over your chin?'

All this, to be appreciated, would have to be written

musically. Orpen's conversation, if one set it to music, would be pitched in the alto clef, marked 'prestissimo,' and accompanied by a sort of Debussy bass, intermittently striking weird gurgly sounds at the most effective moment.

It would also have to be played with an Irish accent, if that were possible. The whole result, at any rate, is very intriguing, especially as Orpen is practically never serious, except when he is working. And then he is a devil.

How we ever really got to business I don't know. I thought 'if all interviewing is like this it will be very charming, and exceedingly fattening, because it apparently necessitates the consumption, on the part of the interviewer, of endless quantities of cucumber sandwiches.'

However, we did do it, and then he let me look at some of his work. There was a picture of a woman (one of the most amusing women in London) on the easel, in a delightful greeny dress.

'How you must have loved painting that dress,' I said.

'Made her put it on.'

'Can you?' And then . . . 'What would you do if a woman with red hair came and sat for you in a purple dress?'

'Make her take it off.'

'But supposing she wouldn't?'

'Take it off myself. Or else show her the door. Couldn't paint that sort of thing. Give me heart attack.'

'What ought red-haired women to wear, then?'

'Green, I should think. Depends on the hair.

Fair-haired women look fine in black. Dark women can wear orange. Anything bright. All this is tripe anyway. Not a dress designer. Could do it, though. Might pay. Bright idea. Have another sandwich?'

As a matter of fact, it would be rather a bright idea if a particularly enterprising dress designer were to pay enormous fees to some artist with a name to come for an hour a day, examine the faces and figures of the clients, and say, 'you ought to wear mauve georgette,' or 'you would look wonderful in jade-green something or other.' Can you imagine John doing it? Or Orpen? The latter would probably say, 'wrap yourself up in a rug and go home.'

'Look at this,' said Orpen. It was the picture of Lord Berkeley which was hung in that year's Academy, a brilliant, sparkling piece of work. 'Nice splosh of colour. Yellow coat. Pink face. Bits of blue. Came off pat. Not everything comes like that.'

It certainly didn't. A friend of mine who has just had his picture done by Orpen said that he painted out the face eleven times before he was satisfied, and then scratched the whole thing because he didn't like the pose.

The next time I saw him – this time unofficially – was just after the discovery of the tomb of Tut-ankh-Amen, when the first photographs of the lovely things inside were beginning to be published in the English papers.

He was standing underneath the great window in his studio, stroking his chin and looking at a full page of illustrations.

149

'My word,' he said, when he saw me, 'What an age to have lived in! Look at that.'

He pointed to the photograph of a lotus vase in perfect condition. Even the reproduction in flat grey colours gave one a thrill which one gets rarely indeed to-day.

'Would you rather have lived with Tut-ankh-Amen than now?' I asked him.

'What questions you ask. Getting better though. Didn't do anything but eat cucumber sandwiches when you first came. Never seen anybody eat so many cucumber sandwiches. Disgusting. Would I what? Rather have lived with Tut-ankh-Amen? Sounds improper. Yes, I should. No other age so stimulating. Lovely lines. *Lovely* lines. Just look at it. Put your nose on it. Eat it.'

And he himself devoured the picture with his own eyes.

We talked a lot about ages we should have liked to live in. I stood up for Venice in the eighteenth century, with Longy's masks and his shadowy ladies who eternally hold their fingers to their lips in dim rooms overlooking some secret canal.

'M'yes. Longy's all right. Damn fine costume. Hides ugly legs. Can't always live at fancy-dress ball though. Jolly interesting to know if an age *was* like what the painters tell us. Middle Ages, now. Wish Renaissance painters hadn't chosen so many Church subjects. One Virgin very like another. Beautiful, of course, but sick of 'em. Think if they'd painted the life around them. Like Rembrandt.'

He got up and started pacing round the room, the alto clef of his voice deepening a little.

'Ever seen Rembrandt's butcher's shop? No? See it. Beauty, beauty, beauty. All out of a lot of meat. No, not out of that. Out of Rembrandt's brain. Doesn't really matter a damn what age you live in if you've got the goods. *There*.' (Tapping his forehead.)

I should think whatever age Orpen had lived in he would have reflected life pretty brilliantly.

'Funny thing, you know,' he added, taking up a tube of ultramarine and sniffing it slightly, 'how one's got to get away from an age quite a long way before you can judge it purely æsthetically. Look at Sargent's picture of that woman, Lady What's-her-name, with the big puffed-out sleeves. Painted in the 'nineties. Damned fine painting. Damned ridiculous dress. You say to yourself, "Lord, what a frump!" In fifty years you'd just look upon it as a design. Can't do that yet. Funny. Earth of the earth, earthy we are.' (Pause.) 'Got blue paint on nose. Why the hell didn't you tell me?'

I left him sitting down on the hearthrug, underneath a bright light, gazing at the photograph of the vase which had once been Tut-ankh-Amen's. I felt quite romantic. 'Perhaps,' I said to myself, 'one of his incarnations had made that vase, and he is seeing in it some of the beauty which he had once realized, and forgotten, and lived again.' Then I remembered the paint on his nose, and laughed.

There is nothing like variety, and journalism certainly gives you that. Soon after the Orpen episode I came in contact with Elinor Glyn, whom one never seems to meet in England except on business.

This lady's appearance is so exactly like that of her own heroines that one can hardly believe she has not just stepped from between the covers of *Three Weeks*. I really have no idea of how I ever was admitted to the presence, for Elinor Glyn has a very good knowledge of the commercial value of her utterances, and is usually so hedged round with Press agents, publishers and literary agents, all waiting to see that her emotions are duly registered, collected, and sold, that there is little chance of gathering anything for nothing. I do not blame Elinor for it. If I had her reputation, I would not express an opinion even on the English climate without demanding a fee, payable in advance.

However, I found myself, one dreary afternoon, in her flat overlooking the Chelsea Embankment. This flat, with two exceptions, contained nothing of the atmosphere which she herself carries with her.

One felt quite sweet and simple in it. A few books, a few rather dull pictures, and an exceedingly upright piano. The two exceptions were, firstly a tiger skin, draped 'negligently' over the sofa, and secondly a pile of cushions, purple and mauve and black. When I saw these, I thrilled. I felt sure that when the authoress entered the room she would leap on to the cushions and begin to talk about life in a hoarse, strangled voice. She entered the room, but she made no sort of attempt to lie on the cushions. On the contrary, she sat straight and still, looked me full in the face, and said, 'Who arranged this?'

I told her that I had not the faintest idea.

She shrugged her shoulders. 'I never give interviews. Still, I suppose it's all right.'

Silence. How deadly a silence can be. Then suddenly, with a charming smile:

'The most terrible people come to see me sometimes. People who ask abominable questions, and look at me as though I were in a cage. You don't appear to do that.'

This interview was turning out to be completely different from anything that I had anticipated. I had come prepared to listen to views on the modern girl, and instead I was treated to a searching cross-examination. Where was my father? Where did I live? I found myself lured by the fascination of those green eyes and orange hair. Suddenly she turned to me and said:

'Do you believe in re-incarnation?'

I gave an evasive answer.

'You should do. You, æons ago, were a horse.'

She may not have used these precise words, but she definitely stated that if my family were traced back sufficiently far, it would eventually prove to be equine in origin.

'And I,' she added, 'come from some cat tribe. Don't laugh.'

She smiled herself, but I think she was serious, for she added: 'The English people completely misunderstand me. They only know things like *Three Weeks* and *The Visits of Elizabeth*. They think of me only as a foolish, sentimental, rather sensual woman. They're blind to the philosophy in me. However – who cares? And anyway, we must get to business. Now what do you want to talk about?'

I gave her a cue – something on the lines of the

153

eternal modern girl, and as soon as she heard that phrase her nostrils quivered, her eyes glared like lamps, her backbone seemed to stiffen like that of a cat on the offensive. And she looked extraordinarily beautiful.

'Women to-day,' she said, 'are revolting men's senses. Look at me. Do *I* slouch into the room, with a guilty look, as though I had not been to bed all night? Do *I* take out a lip stick and slash it over my mouth without caring where it goes? Do *I* daub powder all over my nose until it looks a totally different colour from the rest of my face?'

I answered her that, in our brief but entrancing acquaintance, she had done none of these things.

'Look at my hands.' With a gesture of scorn she held out five very white and exquisite fingers. 'Are *my* hands yellow and horrible through incessantly smoking bad cigarettes?' She leant forward and showed her teeth, looking like some furious goddess. 'Are *my* teeth stained, for the same reason? I ask you? No, they are not.'

She relaxed, but she still looked very grim. 'I can't bear it,' she said, 'this abominable slackness. If I saw my daughters slouching through life like that, I should shoot either myself or them. It is worse in England than anywhere else.'

And then she began to talk about America. 'Perfect dentistry, perfect knowledge of hygiene, and a universal common sense had made the American girl the most wonderful type in the world to-day.' I could see that she adored America. . . .

She said dozens of other things, but I forget them. And one cannot really write about Elinor Glyn, so that I shall stop here and now, leaving this thumb-nail sketch as it stands.

I liked her enormously. If there was ever any occasion on which I found myself forced to use that nauseating word 'queenly,' it would be now. She *is* 'queenly.' She ought to have been born on some dark evening when Balkan thrones were tottering like scenes on the back-cloths of our less draughty London theatres. She ought to have been hustled over the waters of the Ishky-Repoka by faithful nurses, while grizzled prime ministers faced bloody men who demanded a new régime. She ought to have grown up among surroundings of crêpe and asphodels. And then, one day, she ought to have returned in a golden chariot, driven towards a be-flagged palace, walked slowly down immense corri-dors, stood on a throne and started a world-war in a girlish caprice.

It seems a great pity that such a fiery personality should have caused only ink, and not blood, to flow.

CHAPTER FIFTEEN

Concerning Two Artists in a Different Sphere

I HAVE always been puzzled by the universal tendency of democratic communities to attach the most revolting vices to those whom they have chosen to govern them. It is considered a matter of course that the King's Speech should be composed by men in the last stages of delirium tremens. And the majority of Cabinet Ministers are, of course, devotees of such diversions as unnatural vice, unless their fingers are perpetually itching to get at a hypodermic syringe. As an entertainment, one can spend many elevating hours by fixing particular vices to particular ministers, saying, for instance, that President Wilson used to beat his wife, or that Clemenceau had a morning bath of cocaine (which would still not account for his extraordinary vitality). But when one remembers that these libels are uttered with equal assurance by members of every party in the State, the consequent reflection on representative government is not a pleasing one.

Artists are a little luckier than politicians. It is taken for granted, by the great public, that they *must* be immoral, being artists, and their immoralities are not therefore discussed with the same relish. Instead, it is merely asserted that they are mad, a statement which does no harm to anybody.

I wish I could meet these mad artists. Time and again I have been disappointed, and found, instead of straws in the hair, brilliantine, and instead of a foaming mouth, lips pursed in eminently sane and complacent judgment on mankind.

Even when there is some apparent foundation for

the stories, they are always grossly exaggerated. Pachmann, for example. The most astounding tales are constantly narrated about this great little man, how he crawls under the piano in a gibbering search for Chopin, how he is taken from a padded cell and led to the piano by a keeper. Nonsense – or so I judged when, not long before leaving London, I had the pleasure of meeting him.

I had not seen Pachmann since, as a small and evil child, I had once untied his bootlaces under my aunt's piano, on which he used often to perform. His behaviour on that occasion might possibly have strengthened the mad legend, but on our second meeting, though one realized his behaviour was a little odd, nobody but a fool would have thought him mad. Nobody but a fool, indeed, would have failed to be absolutely charmed by his dainty little mannerisms. He danced round the room like some grey-haired Puck, waving his long white fingers on which glittered two beautiful diamond rings. He was always talking nineteen to the dozen, and never finished a sentence. Words seemed too clumsy for him and he would flick his fingers to convey the sense he wanted.

How we laughed and talked! He turned everything to music, even his wine. He held up a glass of champagne to the light, pointing at it and saying – 'Bubbles! Golden, sparkling bubbles! I show you.' And before one could rise to stop him, he had rushed into the darkness of the next room, seated himself at the piano, and played, with magical perfection, a shimmering treble passage from Chopin's Third Scherzo. After which the champagne tasted quite flat.

He told me, after dinner, about one of his early love-affairs, in Poland.

'It was at — ' (some unpronounceable place) he said. 'There was, in the same house as myself, a plump and lovely maiden, oh so beautiful! I fell in love with her a great deal, and one day I arrange a rendezvous. But I forget all about the rendezvous, because I discover a cupboard in which the lady of the house keeps a beautiful collection of jams — I eat the jams and I forget my Louisa. Soon Louisa, she comes into the room and says — "For why have you jilted me? Do you not love me any more?" I take out a plum, and I eat it, and I look at her, and I say, "I love you, Louisa. But I love the jams still better." '

We went into the room which contained his piano, and after a lot more prancing about he suddenly turned to me and said:

'Do you know why I like you?'

I certainly had no idea.

'Because,' said Pachmann, 'you do not ask me to play the piano.'

It would never have occurred to me to do so. But one has to observe that the criminal habit of asking artists out to dine and then expecting them to pay for half-cold entrées by playing or singing, is still quite common, even among otherwise civilized hostesses. Dame Nellie Melba told me that when she first went to New York it was almost unknown for any mere singer to be asked out to dine in any other than a professional capacity. She, of course, had already become almost a royal personage in London, but in New York she was regarded merely as a 'singing

158

actress.' And when, one night, she went to dine with one of the Four Hundred (whatever that absurd phrase means) all the guests whispered:

'What's she going to sing?'

'She isn't going to sing anything at all,' said her host.

'Not going to sing?'

They simply could not understand that a *prima donna* could have any place in society other than that of a *prima donna*.

All of which is a digression from Pachmann. As soon as he had made the remark about not being asked to play, he sat down at the piano and said:

'As a reward I shall play you some Chopin. And I shall play it in two ways. First my old method. Secondly my new.'

He played one of the Chopin Études – not one of the best, but still a very lovely thing. 'That' he said, when he had finished, 'is the old way. Now listen to the new.'

He played it again. I confess that I did not notice much difference. Both were exquisitely played, both had the Pachmann magic, which no other Chopin player has ever been able to find. But that there actually was an astounding difference of technique was demonstrated when, in detail, he played over the first dozen bars. The fingering had been entirely changed, not only in the right hand but in the left.

'That,' he cried triumphantly, 'is the greatest effort of my life. Nobody but Pachmann could have done that.'

He certainly spoke the truth, for nobody but Pachmann could, at his advanced age, have sat down and unlearnt all they had previously learnt, and undertaken the colossal labour of refingering the works of Chopin. It is always more difficult to revise than to attack a thing for the first time, and after sixty, most men would have shuddered at the very thought of it.

Dear Pachmann! I don't think he was very happy in London, although he adored English audiences. London fogs and London smoke stifled him. 'I look out of the window in the morning,' he said, as I bade him good-bye, 'and I weep. And the sky weeps too. And we both weep together. And then, I go and play Chopin, and I weep no more, and the sun shines.'

What dragons they do give the young men of Fleet Street to slay! I heard of one rather timid and bespectacled youth (not in Carmelite House) who had had literary leanings at Cambridge and decided that he would be a writer. He got a job as a reporter on one of the big papers, and the first thing they sent him to do was to ask as many members of the House of Lords as possible what they thought of kissing under the mistletoe. Sick at heart, he departed on his ignoble task, and after sitting for nearly two hours in the corridor that leads to the House of Lords, he summoned up the courage to approach a gentleman who looked harmless enough but who turned out to be the Marquess of Salisbury. He did not get the answer he expected, but the answer he did get sent him rushing down the corridor, terrified, into the open street.

But one does have to ask such very peculiar questions. I once, right at the beginning, was told to go and ask Carpentier if he found it a bore to be so good-looking. A very delicate subject, because it meant asking the complementary question, Would he have liked to be ugly? And one was hearing a great deal, at that time, of Carpentier's straight left.

Fortunately I knew one of Carpentier's best friends, so I routed him out, and he very kindly gave me a letter, in which he first asked 'Georges' to lunch, and then, as a pendant, told him what the bearer of the note desired.

Carpentier was acting in some film or other, and I had to go out to North London to catch him at the studio. After waiting for nearly half an hour in a superbly gilt room, I was led through various passages into the main studio, which rather resembled a huge barn, with a pond in the centre, from which Carpentier had just rescued some maiden who was dripping by the fire. He himself was sitting, an agreeable-looking giant, on the edge of the pond, clad in one of those dressing-gowns which tempt young men in the Burlington Arcade, of purple silk shot with yellow flowers. All round about were supers, and men with lamps, and men with megaphones, and everybody seemed in a very bad temper. Carpentier beckoned me to sit by his side.

As soon as I did so, and presented my note, I was acutely conscious that I was about to ask the heavy-weight champion of Europe a very delicate question, and that I was sitting on the edge of a cold and damp pond, into which a comparatively gentle push would easily have precipitated me. The pond looked so exceedingly wet that I was on the point of changing the interview altogether, and asking him some dull

L

question about his views on boxing, when he turned and, speaking in French, asked me what I wanted.

I told him. Very badly, too.

'Comment?'

Edging slightly away, I repeated the question. 'Did he think good looks were a blessing?'

'Comprends pas,' said Carpentier.

This was terrible. In a very loud voice I said, 'Would he rather have been born "vilain"'?

Now 'vilain' was quite the wrong word to use, because it applies more to the character than to the face. I knew that perfectly well, and as soon as I had said it, realized my mistake. Now, I thought, for the pond! Let's get it over.

'Vilain?' said Carpentier. And then he laughed. Laughed loud and long. So did I. And when he had finished, I at last managed to convey to him exactly what I really did want.

He was extraordinarily amusing. He told me that he was bored silly by the number of females who fell in love with him. As soon as he arrived in England, showers of letters, literally hundreds by each mail, descended on him, some with photographs, some without, some written in terms of passionate adoration, some phrased more discreetly. They did not stop at letters, they spoke to him in the street, they lined up outside the studio. 'Dames de société,' he said, had implored Mr. Stuart Blackton, the producer, that they should be allowed even the smallest walking-on part in the film in order that they might be near their god. All of which, he said, with a charming little shrug of the shoulders, was most tiresome.

'You see,' he said, 'I am married. I have my wife and I have my little daughter. Such things do not amuse me as perhaps – once –' and he smiled in a manner which Noel Coward would describe as winsome.

'But ugly? Oh no. I do not wish to be ugly.'

He drew in a deep breath, and stretched out his arms – so that the dressing-gown slipped down, revealing the figure which had been the cause of all the trouble. A very beautiful creature, I thought. Bodily, not facially. His face is really, when you see it close to, rather coarse. A very thick nose, caused, I suppose, by a bash on it, and a not very imposing forehead. (You see, I am a long way from the pond at the time of writing.) The time he looks best is when he smiles – and that is very often.

I think that Carpentier was quite flattered by his social success, in fact I am sure he was, for he mentioned, rather ingenuously, some places where he had been to parties. It would be interesting to know who was responsible for this, but after all, it was only natural, for everybody wanted him. But he was not always easy to get. For instance, a certain good lady who lives in Arlington Street was giving a party, and was threatened with high blood pressure because she could not get Carpentier. There arrived on the scene an old friend (older than he would like to be thought), who said that he would arrange it. I cannot tell you his name, but he is the original of Mr. Cherrey-Marvel in Michael Arlen's *The Green Hat*. He rushed round London, first to the studio, then to an hotel, then to another hotel, and finally routed out Carpentier just as he was on the point of going to bed. Carpentier said he would not come, because he did not want to dress. 'Don't dress then,' said Cherrey-Marvel, 'but come.'

'Would it be *comme il faut* to come, without even putting on a smoking?'

'Anything would be *comme il faut* that you did,' said Cherrey-Marvel.

And so he went to the party in a lounge suit, and was an enormous success. 'He gives one such a thrill, doesn't he, my dear?' they all said. I expect he would have given them an even greater thrill if he had come in his little blue shorts.

A very charming, unspoilt, simple creature – that was my impression of Carpentier on my first talk with him, and I have not had occasion to alter it since.

CHAPTER SIXTEEN

Hanged by the Neck

In February, 1923, I attended the famous trial of Edith Thompson and Fred Bywaters, which created a sensation in England keener than any which had been felt since the Crippen case.

The first part I had to play in it was to go out, one wet, dreary evening, to North London, to try to persuade Grayson, the father of the murderess on trial, to give me the story of her life. All the other newspapers were on the same job, and it was with a feeling of dismay and depression that I walked down the long sad crescent that led to the Graysons' house, pushed open the rusty little gate, and rang the bell.

The door opened, and the pale face of a little oldish man appeared. He was crying.

'Mr. Nichols?' he said in a voice that was half a whisper.

I nodded.

With a weary gesture he motioned me in. I found myself in a little parlour, neatly kept. It was lit by incandescent gas, which bubbled and fizzled, and cast green shadows in the corners. A little china sparkled on the mantelpiece. There was no fire and the room was very cold.

We sat down. It was all like a nightmare. I could say nothing. He could say nothing. And then his son appeared in the doorway – pale and distracted. Somehow the presence of a third person made it easier, and, rousing myself, I tried to put, as gently as I could, the nature of my request.

He shook his head. It was impossible. All the

papers had been there. They had not had a minute's peace. They could tell them nothing. I passed that over, talking, talking – anything to prevent him again giving way to his grief. And, by and by, he seemed to cheer up a little.

Then, suddenly, without any warning, he threw out his hands, and cried in a broken voice . . . 'To think that this should happen to *us*!'

It was the universal cry of humanity. Why should it happen to *us*? There were five hundred little houses, all exactly alike, in this desolate crescent. There were five thousand equally desolate crescents in London. Why had God picked out *this* one little house out of so many?

The scene passes to the Old Bailey, on which the eyes of all England at this time were centred.

The first sight one has of the Principal Court of Justice at the Old Bailey is not awe-inspiring. It is, of course, a completely modern building, with an air about it which makes it look as though it were designed for a cheerful lecture room at Cambridge. The light wood and plaster, the glass roof, the sunlight that floods the whole place – nothing here to promote any morbid speculations.

But as the court fills, as one by one the barristers take their places at the long tables, as the back benches are occupied by the usual array of stupid women hung with false pearls, as the Judge and jury file into place, and as, finally, the prisoner is led into the dock, then all this cheerfulness, this matter-of-fact atmosphere, this clean, modern feeling, becomes far more horrible than if the trial were conducted in a vault by black inquisitors under candlelight.

For in this place, tragedy is made ridiculous. The mask of pain is moulded into a grotesque. It is almost as though an operation for life or death were taking place before one's eyes, without any anæsthetic. Rather be tried before a howling mob, and bundled straight off in a tumbril to the guillotine, than be brought up to this clean, wholesome room, like a young man undergoing a *viva voce*, in which failure means hanging by the neck.

The court was already packed to suffocation, and I sat down. Five minutes to ten. In a few moments the curtain would rise on the biggest tragedy of 1922. And yet, what was the mood of the audience? Pleasant, amused expectation apparently. From behind me came a whiff of cheap scent and the light chatter of many tongues. Looking up into the gallery one could see the fatuous faces of young girls, wearing the sort of expression you see before the lights go down at a cinema. One of them had a box of chocolates laid on the ledge in front of her, and from time to time she pushed it towards a young man by her side. Standing in the group by the door was a very bad and very popular actor, bowing ceremoniously to the scented ladies. The only people who looked at all serious were the police, and one felt that they were serious only because they had duties to perform.

Ten o'clock. The curtain rises. I shut my eyes. There is a mumble of voices, a shuffling of feet, a rustle of papers. Silence. I open my eyes again to find that the 'female prisoner' is already in the dock, and that the play has begun.

Look at her, this 'female prisoner.' Look at her,

this Edith Thompson, *née* Grayson, who has spent twenty-eight passionate, unhappy years on this earth, and is now being sent to eternal darkness. (I am drifting irresistibly into the style of Carlyle, but I can't help it.) A lovely creature, one would say. A neck like the stem of a flower, and a face equally flower-like. So very white, with the pallor of old lilies carved in ivory. So very tired, as though no longer could that one head support the burden of so much pain.

Oh yes. I know that she is a murderess. I know that she is an adulteress. That foully, and with felonious intent, she did, on divers occasions attempt to do to death an honest and an upright man. I know all that, and a good deal more besides. But I also know that my heart is wrung with pity.

A man with a red face is cross-examining her. He leans forward, and reads from a letter in his hand. It is one of those amazing love-letters which this strange creature had sent from her dingy suburb to her boy lover.

Your love to me is new, it is something different, it is my life, and if things should go badly with us, I shall always have this past year to look back upon and feel that 'then I lived.' I never did before and never shall again.

Darlingest lover, what happened last night? I don't know myself, I only know how I felt — no, not really how I felt, but how I could feel — if time and place or circumstances were different.

It seems like a great welling up of love, of feeling, of inertia, just as if I am wax in your hands to do with as

168

*you will, and I feel that if you do as you wish I shall be
happy. I can't really describe it — but you will understand, darlint, won't you? You said you knew it would
be like this one day — if it hadn't would you have been
disappointed?*

And again, when he was far away:

*I've nothing to talk about darlint, not a tiny little thing.
Life — the life I and we lead is gradually drawing
near. Soon, I'll be like the Sahara — just a desert
'Shulamite.' You must read that book — it's interesting,
absorbing. Aren't books a consolation and a solace?
We ourselves die and live in the books we read while we
are reading them, and when we have finished, the books
die and we live or exist. Just drag on thro' years and
years until when? Who knows? I'm beginning to think
no one does — not even you and I. We are not the shapers
of our destiny. I will always love you, darlint.*

I found myself longing for their escape, planning
for it, wondering if by some miracle it could not be
brought about. The main well of the court is sur-
mounted by a glass roof. If only, I thought, some
friend could land on that roof in an aeroplane, shatter
the glass with a single blow, throw down a rope to
the two tortured creatures in the dock, and pull
them up, up, out of this hell into the clean air above.
If only there would be an earthquake to rend the
walls, so that this gloating crowd would rush away
affrighted, and leave the lovers to themselves. If
only there would be an utter darkness, to cover all
this shame, and set us free. Bad reasoning of course,
on my part. Bad sociology. Bad law. Justice has to

be done, and all that sort of thing. But I defy any sensitive person to sit through a long trial of this description, to see a beautiful woman and a strong young man slowly done to death, without siding, heart and soul, with the accused.

During the whole of that tragic trial, through gloom to deepening gloom, I was in constant touch with the Grayson family. As I saw more of them, I marvelled that so utterly commonplace and kindly a group of individuals should have, as one of their members, the complex, passionate character of Edith Thompson. The mother I hardly recollect, save as a little, broken woman in black, whose hand was always to her eyes and who walked with uncertain steps, as though stumbling in darkness. But there was a sister whom I often saw. She seemed to have more control over herself than any other member of the family. She was cool, almost dominating, in the witness-box, and in her own home she was the one who assumed the chief burden of work and responsibility. A brother, too, I remember, with a face drained of all colour and eyes red with secret weeping. As for Grayson himself, he was just stunned. There is no other word which adequately describes his slow, mumbling speech, his downcast eyes, his dumb look of pain.

At three o'clock on Saturday afternoon during the trial, I used to meet Grayson as he came out of Holloway Prison. Do you know Holloway Prison? It is of all places the most dreary and forlorn. It lies at the end of the long and dismal Caledonian Road in North London. It has no colour save the faded advertisement hoardings which peel from the dirty walls, no animation but for the noisy trams that rattle down the end of the street, and the cries of pale children playing in the gutter.

The prison itself is built of grey stone, like a fortress. It has narrow windows and high walls. Over the whole pile broods an air of monstrous cruelty and strength, from the rusted spikes that guard the outer wall's summits to the heavy gates that shut out its inmates from the world. I would stand watching these gates for five minutes, ten minutes, half an hour, and then they would swing slowly open and through them would emerge the little sombre procession, Grayson, the brother – sometimes the sister and the mother as well.

Silently I would join them and walk with them down the road, while the trams rattled by, and the newsboys shouted out the latest details of the case, and lovers jostled us, arm-in-arm. And then the cross-examination would begin.

'How was she?'

'She was better. Brighter.'

'Were you allowed to go into her room?'

'No. They put a table across the door. We spoke to her over that. We stood in the corridor. There was a warder by her side.'

'What was she wearing?'

'A dressing-gown. You see, she's been in bed. Ill. Very ill. Exhausted, they say. Still, she was better, and she has been reading.'

'What books has she been reading?'

'Dickens, she told us. She said that she wanted life and comedy, and Dickens gave her that. Full-blooded life – that was the word she used.'

'Did she say anything about – him?'

'Him?'

'Yes. Bywaters?'

'No. His name never crossed her lips. She asked about her appeal, and she seemed quite hopeful about it. And then – she began to remember things.'

'Remember things?'

'Yes. Last Christmas for example. She said "Do you remember the party we had last Christmas? And all the presents I had? And the crackers? And the Christmas tree?" '

And then I would shake them by the hand, and wish them good cheer, and say that I was sure the appeal would turn out right – anything to take away that look of tragedy from their eyes. They would brighten, perhaps, for a moment, and then the mask would fall over their faces again, as they turned away, and went down the windy street.

The most horrible meeting of all, as far as I was concerned, was on the day after she had been hanged. I was in the office, writing some ridiculous account of an agricultural exhibition, when word was brought that Grayson wished to see me.

It was the most difficult thing I have ever had to do. I found him sitting in the waiting-room, under a glaring electric light. Standing by his side, with one hand on his shoulder, was the son. We looked at each other in silence. What was there to say? What language was ever invented which could possibly be fitted to an occasion so forlorn?

Eventually we did speak – or rather, I spoke. 'Bit knocked up,' was all he could say. 'Bit knocked up.' Over and over again, like a child repeating a lesson it had learnt and did not understand. I told him that they must all go away to the country, to the sea, anywhere, as long as they were away from prying eyes, from the memory of the dead.

He went out. 'Bit knocked up,' he said again, and that was the last I heard of him.

CHAPTER SEVENTEEN

Two Plain and One Coloured

QUITE the most amusing person I met at about this time was H. L. Mencken, whose books *Prejudices* so perfectly describe the particular standpoint in art which he has adopted. We met, as far as I remember, at some party or other at the Café Royal, but as it was impossible to talk in that establishment, under the distracting influence of Epsteins, Augustus Johns, Laverys and successive glasses of absinth, we arranged to meet the next morning at his hotel. 'And then I'll give you something that'll wake you up.'

He did. And it did. When I called on him he was tramping backwards and forwards in his rooms, making a strange spluttering noise with his lips that suggested a large and angry bird stalking round its cage. After refusing the inevitable double whisky which Americans apparently seem to consider an hourly necessity for Englishmen, I asked him what was the matter.

'Matter?' Again the spluttering noise, this time a little louder. 'I've just been looking at London. What the devil are you doing to it? Do you want to make it another New York? A filthy sky-scraper in the Strand, half the most exquisite buildings being scrapped and thrown on to the muck heap, and obscene advertising signs that are as bad as anything we've got on Broadway.'

Splutter, splutter, splutter.

I thought it would be a good idea to ask him what he would do if he were suddenly given despotic powers over the reconstruction of London.

'The first thing I'd do,' he said, lighting a cigar with a sort of aggressive courage that reminded one of firing a torpedo, 'would be to hang every mother's son of an architect who was polluting one of the world's best cities. And when they were dangling high and dry, I'd go out with a packet of dynamite, blow up all the monstrosities in Regent Street, get hold of Nash's old plans, and slave-drive a few thousand British navvies until we'd got the thing back as it used to be – a superb crescent, full of grace and beauty.'

Splutter, splutter, splutter.

He resumed his perambulation round the room. 'Then I'd invent a whole lot of brand-new tortures for any hulking Philistine of a manufacturer who started writing his blasted name on God's sky at night. Piccadilly Circus nowadays is an eyesore. It's bad enough in Broadway. But you can at least say there that the vast scale on which the signs are put up, the enormous size of the whole thing, does at least leave a certain feeling of awe on one's mind. Disgust too, but at least, *big*. Whereas in Piccadilly you've got a lot of footling little electric squares and circles, a yellow baby spitting fire, an undersized motor squiggling its wheels, a God-forsaken bottle pouring red liquid into a glass so damned small that it wouldn't make me tight if I drank out of it all night. Take 'em away!' (Splutter, splutter.) 'Take 'em away! You're killing London!'

I think I have got in most of his adjectives. His conversation was also scattered with a good many examples of that word which Bernard Shaw employed with such effect in *Pygmalion*. These I have omitted.

He went on for some time in this strain, until I felt it time to point out to him that at least we were putting up a few new buildings that were quite worthy to stand by the old ones.

'Show 'em to me!' (Splutter, splutter.) 'Take me along to see 'em. I'll stand you drinks for a month if what you say is true.'

'Well, there's the new L.C.C. building on the other side of the Thames. Knott's the architect. One of the biggest buildings of its kind in the world, and one of the most beautiful.'

He looked at me despairingly. 'Oh, you ought to have been an American if you say a monstrosity like that's beautiful. I looked at it yesterday, and I spat in the Thames to show my contempt of it.'

'But the line of it is perfect — the proportions are admirable . . .'

'Perfect rot. For one thing, what on earth induced the fool who built it to stick a hulking great red roof on top of it? All down that side of the Thames is grey. Grey old buildings, peering out of the mist, like veiled faces, tumble-down old ruins, wharfs, docks, bridges, grey, all grey. And then this fool comes along and sticks up a blasted Noah's Ark, covered with pillars and crowned with this futile roof. What's the good of that?'

I told him that if he were a real Londoner, he might not be so angry at the sight of an occasional touch of colour. He might not be so keen on his universal touch of grey if he had to live in it for ever. He might, if he had to cross the Thames day by day, year by year, come to welcome that red roof, sparkling across the grey water, and bringing even into the dullest days a glow of cheerfulness, as of reflected sunshine.

But he would have none of it. The roof should have been grey, and that was an end to the matter. I understood then why he had written three books called *Prejudices*.

None the less, a charming man, who is more American than he would care to think, for all his constant nagging at his own country. I said something vaguely derogatory of a certain section of American opinion, and he was down on me like a shot. I liked him best at that moment.

One of the most tiresome things I ever had to do was – Rudolph Valentino.

It was only after hours of ringing up and fixing appointments, over which more trouble was spent than if he had been an Arch-Duchess, that I eventually was told I could see him one morning at ten o'clock at the Carlton Hotel. The Carlton Hotel, in fact any hotel, is sufficiently depressing at ten o'clock in the morning, and when I discovered that Valentino, instead of giving a private appointment, was standing in the centre of a circle of admiring females, telling them, I should imagine, a lot of nonsense, I felt like going straight away and leaving him to his own devices.

However, after a time, I got him into a corner, and by carrying on the conversation in atrocious French, kept the subject of most our remarks a secret from 50 per cent of the said females. Unfortunately there proved to be nothing to keep secret. 'Did he get many letters?' 'Yes, he got three thousand a week.' 'Were there many letters from adorers?' 'They all adored him.' 'What sort of letters?' 'He never read them.' And so on. He could say nothing as to whether he was elated by his success, he had no sort of theories, not even bad ones, on the film as a medium of art, and he was without a spark of humour in his composition. This is the most adored man throughout two continents.

The only subjects in which he seemed to be at all interested were, firstly, his own photographs, and secondly, clothes. Of photographs there were literally hundreds, lying scattered all over the room. He pointed to a pile and said, 'These go off by the next mail.' Surely he saw some romance in that? I tried to get him to understand the thrill that most people would have at the thought of their own faces smiling down from ten thousand London mantel-pieces and bringing, presumably, a disturbing ecstasy into the hearts of ten thousand maidens. He merely looked blankly at me and said he supposed it was good publicity.

But when it came to discussing the photographs themselves it was a very different matter. Did I like this one looking down, or did I prefer the one looking up? Would the chin be a little better if it were switched round more to the right, and did I not think that the eyes had come out beautifully in that one? Yes, I said, the chin *was* nicely switched, and the eyes *had* come out beautifully. Upon which he brightened considerably, and offered me a photograph for myself, which I declined.

The only thing we had in common appeared to be a tailor. He asked me if I had heard of any good tailors (not if I *went* to a good one, a rather intriguing difference) and I told him that I always went to a certain place, which made clothes that appeared to fit, and also gave one as much credit as anybody could reasonably desire. 'Why, that's where I'm going myself,' he said. 'How extraordinary.'

He certainly did know a great deal about clothes, as I discovered later when a man from the firm in question called on me one morning with some new and demoralizing stuffs from Paris. He had just finished cutting three new double-breasted grey flannel suits for Valentino, and had evidently met a kindred spirit.

I should imagine that half Valentino's success (once one has acknowledged the purely sensual attraction of his face and his shapely limbs) came from his wife. A very beautiful creature, I thought her, with a vivacity and a sparkle that Valentino himself will never have.

Of caricaturists there are legion, but I never met one even vaguely resembling the genius that is 'Sem.' Sem is, of course, famous all over France, and in a good many other countries as well. Queens of every description have screamed when they opened his portfolio, and they tell me that as soon as the Aga Khan heard that he was one of Sem's victims, his knees clattered together in soft and mutual sympathy. For some reason, however, he is not so well known in England, though, naturally enough, many lovely ladies have unsuccessfully offered enormous sums, if only Sem would make them sufficiently ridiculous.

You would not think, when you met him, that Sem 'had it in him' to be so very naughty. Such a tiny little man, rather like an amiable monkey, with a small wizened face, and eyes that blink perpetually in a sort of mild surprise at the fantastic comedy of life. It is only when his face suddenly sets, and his neck cranes forward, that you realize that here is a man who sees more than you would even imagine there was to be seen.

It was just after the publication of one of his most sensational folios that we met. I wanted to know how he did it – a sufficiently comprehensive question to ask any artist.

'Do you go about with a pencil and paper, looking for monstrosities?' I asked him. 'Getting a nose here, a neck there, a double chin somewhere else?'

He shook his head emphatically. 'Never do I draw a line from life,' he asserted. 'I look at people when they do not know that they are being watched. At Deauville, when they are plunging into the water, in the theatre, when they are excited by the stage, at dinner, when they are excited by the soup. At times like that they forget that they must make the best of themselves. The large women forget to hide their chins, the large men forget to be dignified. That is the time for me. But I do not *draw*, then. Oh no! I wait a week, a month, six months. And suddenly I think, that woman, she was like a horse, or that fellow, he resemble a camel. Then, I draw.'

One of his caricatures which had struck me as most delightful was that of Lady Idina Gordon, whom he saw as a heron, and whom everybody will see as a heron for the rest of her natural life.

'Yes,' he said. 'I say, that is a heron, as soon as she comes. Very English. Head so. Neck so. And the voice. Just like I draw. And the Aga Khan? You see him like a fish too, like me? All of a fishiness, I see him, with the large eyes and the mouth.' He made an exquisite little grimace to illustrate his meaning.

'And the King of Spain? They say I am rude to draw him so, but it is not rudeness. It is only Truth. I draw them as I see them. I do not make a monkey of a lion, nor a peacock of a sparrow.'

And yet, Sem can be kind as well as cruel. He dips his pen alternately in poison and soothing syrup, and draws, first with a knife and then with a caress. His curly, twisting nib worms right into the heart of his subject, dragging out the most astonishing intimacies. A twist of the lip and he has condemned not only an individual but a whole class. A swelling of the stomach and the whole monstrous regiment of profiteers stands shameless before you.

He didn't seem much impressed by English caricaturists. Even after his second Bronx, the mention of Max Beerbohm merely drew a sigh from his lips and a little flick of the monkey fingers. 'There is nothing much about him,' he said. 'He is not a caricaturist. He is a commentator. His drawing is not strong enough to stand alone, and so he must put little bubbles into the mouths of his characters, and make them speak for him. That is amusing' (and here he nibbled his moist cherry much as monkeys nibble peanuts at the Zoo) 'but it is not caricature.'

He swallowed the cherry and, leaning forward, burst into French. 'Caricature,' he said, 'must stand by itself. It must have a line that shatters, a cut that kills. There must be no mists, no legends, no little sentences stuck here and there to say "this is a fool." You must *draw* him as a fool, and your very *line* must be foolish, it must wriggle with absurdity, it must twist itself remorselessly into the grotesque. There is only one man in England who can do that to-day.'

'And who is that?' I asked.

'Bateman. Mr. H. M. Bateman. Now he has no need to put balloons into the mouths of his characters. They speak for themselves. They laugh out loud. He is a great caricaturist, that man. He could kill a man with a single drop of ink.'

He leant back and closed his eyes. Poor Sem has bad eyes, and he blinks, not through astonishment, as I first surmised, but because a strong light hurts him. All round us surged the highly coloured and slightly ridiculous set of people who are always to be seen drifting through the lounges of London's three hotels at cocktail time. Women whose complexions all come out of the same sort of bottle, men whose clothes all come from the same sort of tailor. The same tired voices, the same overfed stomachs, the same underfed intelligences. Immediately in front of us was a much *soignée* lady in black – dress by Molyneux, diamonds by Cartier, furs by Reville, perfume, I should imagine, by request. I wished that Sem would look at her.

But he was already looking at her. 'I shall draw her,' he said, 'as a cat.'

And he did.

CHAPTER EIGHTEEN

A Lamb in Wolf's Clothing

I NOW retired to a nursing home for an operation. The operation had nothing to do with my visit to Valentino, for it was only 'tonsils' – and I spent my few days of rest in reading *Main Street*, which had a very cheering effect by making one remember how many disagreeable people there were in the world with whom it was not necessary to live.

One afternoon I was deep in the atmosphere of the Middle West when I looked up and saw, standing in the doorway, a youth with fair hair, agreeable features, quizzical smile, and appalling clothes.

'Who are you?' I said.

'I'm Oliver Baldwin,' replied the apparition.

Now, Oliver Baldwin is, to the best of one's knowledge, a figure unique in English history, and as biographies will certainly be written about him when he is old and respectable there seems every reason for writing something about him while he is young and – Oliver,

Oliver's father is, of course, Prime Minister. But Oliver himself was and is the most violent revolutionary, with a considerable flair for public speaking, a complete independence of thought, and an absolute loathing for his father's Party.

England was therefore presented with the engaging spectacle of a young man filling the bookshelves of Number 11 Downing Street with treatises on the best way to blow up Cabinet Ministers. In fairness to Oliver it should be observed that he only did this while his father was Chancellor of the Exchequer.

In the more exalted days of the present he avoids Downing Street like the plague.

In spite of the discouragement of tonsils we were very soon talking with gusto.

'Does your father mind your wanting to be the President of the First English Republic?' I asked him.

'I don't know. Never asked him.'

'But isn't it – don't you think it's rather . . . I mean . . .' (Impossible to finish this sentence.)

Oliver smiled. 'You mean, don't I think it's bad form to attack my own papa in public? No. The only things which are bad form are the things which are not sincere. I am terribly sincere. And I'm not attacking *him*, I'm attacking the programme he stands for.'

More talk, Oliver departed, and it was arranged that we should meet again.

In the meanwhile I found out a little more about Master Baldwin which made me realize that he was a person with whom, one day, we should be forced to reckon. Before his exploits the adventures of Huckleberry Finn pale into insignificance. After a cloistered youth in the shadow of Eton, he suddenly, at the outbreak of war, enlisted in the Second Cambridge Cadet Corps, became a sergeant-instructor, an officer in the Irish Guards, went through France, and was a seasoned warrior before he was out of his teens. The war over, he departed to Russia to fight the Bolsheviks, was imprisoned by these gentlemen for months under sentence of death, escaped, got into Armenia, avoided meeting Mr. Michael Arlen, grew (with infinite pains) a beard, joined the Armenian army, became in rapid succession a Captain, Major, Colonel, General, bought a white horse, and led, like a new Joan of Arc, the army of the Armenians against the Bolsheviks. All these things – even the beard – probably had singularly little effect on the course of events, but they showed the stuff of which Oliver was made.

Oliver is not in the least the vulgar tub-thumper of popular imagination. He is almost absurdly sensitive about his position. I remember motoring down from London to Oxford with him once, coming within a few miles of Chequers, and demanding firmly to be driven there at once. 'Do you think we ought to?' he said. 'Why not?' said I. 'There won't be any Cabinet Ministers there, and even if there are, they can't bite us. I rather wish they could. It would be fun to be bitten by the Chancellor of the Exchequer.'

So we went to Chequers, simply because I shamelessly insisted.

We arrived when it was still early morning, with the mist of an English autumn drifting down the lanes and lying, like a caress, over the little green fields. What a paradise! When the Lee's left it to the Prime Ministers of England, they must have been thinking of future Labour governments, because this old place is so peaceful, so mellow, so typical of all that is gracious and lovely in English history (as we fondly imagine it to have been), that nobody could dwell within its walls for more than a few hours without wishing to preserve the spirit which had created it.

I won't give a catalogue of the treasures of Chequers, because they would fill a whole volume, from the magnificent Rembrandt which dreams in the dusk of the tall entrance hall to the marvellous collection of unique volumes which line the shelves of the long, quiet library. What most appealed to one was the entire absence of any 'museum' feeling, all the more remarkable when one remembers that Chequers belongs to the nation, and is only a temporary resting-place for successive ministers.

Nothing is locked up under glass cases. Looking back on it, I think that it might be just as well if some of the things were protected. For example when Oliver was not looking, I put a ring of Queen Elizabeth on my finger (she must have had very large fingers), clasped a sword of Oliver Cromwell's in my hand and read aloud the original Cromwell letter in which he describes the rout of the Cavaliers as 'God made them as stubble to our swords.' The combined effect of all these actions gave one a feeling that was a cross between a museum and the worst type of tourist.

At Chequers there is a very charming lady who occupies the post of châtelaine, and who could probably tell more secrets than any other woman in Europe, for she has seen all the Prime Ministers in their moments of play and rest, when they have been most likely to tell the truth. However, she is discretion itself, and when one asked if Lloyd George ever said what he really thought about Asquith, or if any of the Prime Ministers ever got drunk, one was met with an evasive smile. However, I did learn later, from another source, that they were all passionately devoted to Chequers itself. In fact, as soon as the news of Lloyd George's downfall came through, Megan Lloyd George, who was in the entrance hall at the time, walked disconsolately to the window, looked out over the moonlit garden, and said, 'Oh dear! This means that we shall have to leave Chequers.' The thought of that, you see, had eclipsed even the disaster which had befallen her father.

Another thing which one realized while at Chequers was the insatiable passion of British Prime Ministers for music. In the great banqueting hall (where nobody banquets now) is a pianola. The first thing which harassed Premiers always did was to rush to this pianola, switch it on, and lie back, forgetting the trials of office. Lloyd George, whose natural taste would seem, to the uninitiated, to be for marches and military music, found himself most soothed by Chopin nocturnes. Baldwin, on the other hand, invariably played, as his first number, some Schubert variations on a theme by (I believe) Mozart. Winston Churchill had the best taste of the lot. He confined himself rigorously to Beethoven.

The surroundings of Chequers are ideally beautiful. On one side, level meadows, on the other, rising hills, thickly wooded. As soon as we had 'done' Chequers, we motored away, got out again, and went for a walk in these woods. And there, under the yellowing leaves of immemorial elms, like the two thoroughly shameless young men that we were, improvised a debate in which Oliver was the President of the First English Republic, and I was the leader of the fast vanishing and decadent English aristocracy — rôles of singular charm for both of us.

The subject was a fantastic one, being concerned with a Bill brought in by the government to requisition all the sticks and leaves in the country for the purpose of burning the House of Lords. Still, it gave us endless opportunities for rhetoric, and as our words floated out into the valley, I wondered if there would ever come a time when the scene would be transferred to the realms of reality. I should imagine that it is most unlikely.

CHAPTER NINETEEN

Two Big Men and One Medium

RUDYARD KIPLING is a fine example of a great man who will forgive almost everything to Youth. He certainly forgave me as charmingly as it was possible to do so.

It happened during lunch. I felt very guilty when they said that Rudyard Kipling was coming, because two years before, when still at Oxford, I had written a letter to the *Morning Post* on the subject of 'Our Modern Youth,' in which there were a great many violent (and rather silly) remarks levelled against anybody who had the misfortune to be over forty. The letter attacked, with sublime indifference, such diverse subjects as militarism, old age, imperialism, prime ministers and incidentally Kipling, whom I had never read, but who seemed to sum up a great many aggressive tendencies. 'Where,' I asked, in the peroration, 'will you find the spirit of the age? Not in the flamboyant insolence of Rudyard Kipling, not in the . . . etc.'

Not one of my best works, that letter. But it was written in a hammock, on a hot summer's day, with flies buzzing round, and certainly without the thought that perhaps, one day, the writer would meet the man whom he had attacked.

However, when Kipling was announced, he came straight up to me (where I was hiding in a corner) and said:

'You're the young man who was so rude to me in the *Morning Post*, aren't you?'

I admitted that this was so. 'I'm awfully sorry . . .' I began.

'Sorry? What for?' said Kipling. 'I used to be much ruder to people when I was your age. The only thing that I should be sorry for was that you didn't make it worse.'

I heaved a sigh of relief.

'Besides,' said Kipling, 'that was a jolly good phrase – flamboyant insolence – I liked it.'

And then he began to talk about literary style with a gusto that is more often found in amateurs than in celebrities.

Kipling did not strike one, in the very least, as 'literary.' If one had not seen his face caricatured in a hundred newspapers, one would gather that he was a successful surgeon or a prosperous architect. Especially does he convey the surgeon, with his keen bright eyes, his more-than-bedside manner, and the strong, capable hands, that push out eagerly from the white cuffs as though they were about to carve something.

Carving, too, is a phrase that might be applied to his prose. He hacks out his sentences, cuts up his paragraphs, snips at his descriptions.

I was struck, even at the beginning, with his positively encyclopædic knowledge of subjects about which he might well have pleaded justifiable ignorance. Drugs, for example. Somebody mentioned anæsthetics, and that led to a wider discussion of all drugs that partially or wholly remove consciousness. Kipling suddenly broke into the conversation, held it and dominated it, illustrating everything he said with the most apposite examples. He told me that when he was in India, as a young man, he had experimented in taking a very potent drug which even the natives can only imbibe in small quantities. 'It laid me out completely,' he said, 'and I didn't dream a bit, as I had hoped. I woke up, with a splitting headache, but fortunately I knew the cure – hot milk, as much of it as you can drink. If ever you find yourself in that condition in India, you put your last dollar on hot milk. It's the only thing that will pull you round.'

It was an amusing luncheon party, for everybody talked about the things that most interested them. I remember Princess Alice,[1] for example, talking about Bolshevism with an authority and an understanding that came to me as rather a surprise.

'How do you know so much about these things?' I asked.

'I think it's my duty to know about them' she said. And then . . . 'I *must* tell you the story of when I went down to speak at a meeting at Poplar. Poplar at the time was seething with Bolshevism, and everybody said it was madness for me to go. To make matters worse, just before the meeting I received a message to say that the whole audience were going to wear red rosettes to show their revolutionary sympathies. Very well, said I, I'll wear a red rosette too. So I got my maid to make me a beautiful scarlet rosette, and pinned it to my dress, where it looked charming. It quite took the wind out of their sails when they saw me get up on the platform wearing exactly the same emblem as themselves. And there wasn't any Red Flag sung that night – only God Save the King, rather out of time, but with a great deal of fervour, all the same.'

[1] Countess of Athlone.

Another rare type I met just then was Sir Thomas Lipton, whose yachts have floated all over the sea, and whose tea has floated into every interior. He wanted me to do a job of work for him, and though I had a shrewd suspicion that there would never be time to do it, I kept my appointment, simply in order to see what he was like.

Lipton himself was charming. And I admired his courage in decorating his house in a manner which some might find disturbing, but which he liked. There was no compromise with modernity. It was frankly Victorian.

From the outside the house looked quite innocuous. It was one of those roomy, squarely built mansions, that stand in respectable gardens on the outskirts of North London. But the porch showed a true individuality. It contained two highly glazed yellow pots, filled with aspidistras, standing on a floor of coloured tiles.

As soon as one entered the hall the fun began. There were black china negresses, 'nice bright' wallpapers, heads of healthy animals, glazed oleographs, and at every turn, photographs of some royalty in a large silver frame. One object in the billiard-room I particularly admired. This was a sofa, covered with cushions of really inspiring colours. One cushion, which was placed between a blue and orange stripe and a form of black check, had for its main design the Star-spangled Banner, worked in blue and crimson wools.

Conversation amid such surroundings was bound to be exciting. Lipton got under way, and let flow an apparently inexhaustible stream of reminiscences.

There was something very appealing in listening to the candid confessions of an entirely self-made multi-millionaire, who gloried in the fact that he *was* self-made.

Lipton told me that he was the first English tradesman who really understood advertising.

'When I got my first little shop,' he said, speaking with a beautiful Scottish burr, 'I realized two things: first, that if you wanted to sell more goods than the man next door, you had to sell better goods. Secondly, that if you wanted to sell a *great many* more goods, you had to make people look at 'em, whether they wanted to or not.

'D'you know what I did?' And here he slapped his thigh and chuckled to himself, 'I got hold of two fat pigs, painted "Lipton's Orphans" on their backs, and used to lead 'em home from the market-place every day. That was good advertising, wasn't it?'

I agreed.

'But even better's to come, even better's to come!' (Here the secretary departed, and I had a suspicion that he had heard the story before.) 'I trained those pigs to lie down in the middle of the road just opposite my wee shop! Think of it. Two braw pigs lying down like that. They stopped the traffic. When we got a crowd round, somebody would say "Why! *There's* the wee shop!" And they'd all trot along and look at my window. What d'you think of that?'

And then he told me the story of Lipton's Bank Notes – almost the best piece of publicity that can ever have been invented. One of his chief slogans was: 'Lipton gives £1 value for 15s.,' or something to that effect, and in order to spread this slogan all over England he had £1 notes issued with a note in very small type at the bottom that goods to the value of £1 could be bought for only 15s. at any of Lipton's stores. So beautifully were these notes engraved that occasionally they would be used, by canny and dishonest persons, in place of the real article. The authorities learnt this and Lipton had to stop his notes. But not before several little comedies had occurred.

'D'you know,' said Sir Thomas, with a sparkle in his eye, 'that a man in an hotel at Edinburgh actually gave me one of my own notes as part of my change? Did I what? No, I didn't. He was a clever fellow, and I let him keep it.

And . . .' here he leant back in a sudden paroxysm of mirth, 'I was travelling in the train once with two elders and they were talking of the collection at the Kirk the Sabbath before.

' "Five pounds seventeen and elevenpence," said one of 'em.

' "Aye," said the other, "but three of the notes were Liptons." '

Lipton has, of course, a real veneration for Kings and Queens. He adores them with a fervour that at times almost becomes poetical, and he can never quite rid himself of the shy wonder that he, the ex-factory boy who started life on 2s. 6d. a week, should have risen to such heights.

He took me into his drawing-room (which I believe he called a parlour) and showed me some of his collection of royal photographs, with the remark that:

'No other commoner in the United Kingdom has ever entertained the same number of crowned heads.'

Looking at the photographs, I could quite believe it. Royal photographs are all very well in small numbers, but in quantities they become a little oppressive. There were several rows of them on the piano, all in heavy silver frames, there were pictures of Queen Victoria on the wall, slightly fly-blown, there were portraits of King Edward, stout and urbane, on the mantelpiece, and every table had on it a photograph of some high-busted lady or be-whiskered gentleman, signed Augusta or Charles or Emelia or John, or some such name, with the signature written in that curious scrawl which denotes either a royal origin, success behind the footlights, or delirium tremens.

And yet – Lipton himself was still simple and charming. His pride was so naïve that one could not possibly object to it. 'The Kaiser said to me . . .' 'Her Majesty remarked . . .' 'The Prince of Wales and I . . .' – they were all only little pats on the back of the ex-factory boy.

Even when he said to me:

'I've the largest collection of Press cuttings in the whole world,' the remark seemed, by the way in which it was said, to be in the best of taste.

The quality which I found most lovable about Sir Thomas Lipton was his intense devotion to his mother. That was the only time when he was really serious. He told me that all his life he had worked for her and for her alone, and that he had never found any other woman in the world who could make him forget her. And his very last words to me were:

'You stick to your mother, laddie, as you would stick to life. As long as you do that, you won't go far wrong.'

I don't know what it is about Hugh Walpole that I find, no doubt wrongly, a little worrying, unless it is his appearance of complacency. He *is* so successful, isn't he? I have really no right to mention him at all, for I only met him once, and that was at a station, when we were both 'seeing off' a mutual friend to America – a situation which was sufficient to make enemies of us for life. But I had heard – oh, a great deal about him from the friend in question, who was a very delightful American woman who has been fairy godmother to a great many young authors and artists.

We were in Venice together (the very delightful American woman and I) and one day she said, 'Let's go and get some lemons for Hugh Walpole.'

'Lemons? They'll go bad long before we get home.'

'Not real lemons. Glass apples. Venetian glass. Hugh has taken a new house in London and I want to give him a present.'

So we entered a gondola, pushed off across the silver water, and were soon in Salvati's, buying beautiful glass lemons for Hugh.

If this is to be a history of my life, as it is rapidly appearing to become, I had better get the subject of Venetian glass off my chest at once. It used to drive me quite mad with excitement, and still does – in

Venice. On the morning in which the very delightful American woman and I went in search of the
lemons, a new and most divine set of glass had just
come in fresh from the factory. There were pieces of
yellow glass that were like frozen sunlight, shadowy
goblets that seemed to be bubbles poised on a puff
of smoke, dim bowls that might just have been taken
dripping from the green depths of the sea, pots of
plain, clean glass with tiny fruits in sharp colours on
the tops, little twinkling plums and vivid sour green
apples. There were rich goblets engraved with
golden dragons, and tall slim cups of grey glass, like
pale ladies coming out of a mist.

We chose our lemons, entered the gondola, and
drifted down the grand canal. I did not particularly
want to hear about Hugh Walpole, but he was
apparently 'in the air,' so I asked why he was so
great a success in America.

'Because they think he's typically English. They
also think he's exceeding clever,' said the very
delightful American woman (who may be referred to
as the V.D.A.W.).

'But he's neither.'

'How do you know? You've never met him' (which
was perfectly true). 'He *is* typically English. His
face is like an old English squire's. And he is very
clever. Or at least we think so.'

And then the V.D.A.W. delivered herself of a very
good piece of literary criticism.

'You'll find Hugh Walpole's books in every best
bedroom in the United States, except possibly, in
the very best ones, where you will not find works in
English but in French, to show that we have trav-

elled. Way out in the middle West, there will be a copy of *The Dark Forest* or *The Prelude to Adventure* carefully placed on a table near the radiator. It will probably never have been read, but it will be there. That's culture.'

An extraordinary idea. 'How does one get this reputation for culture?' I said. 'My books have just as nice covers as Hugh Walpole's, and there is no reason why they should not also have the benefit of steam heat.'

'You're too young,' was the only answer I got.

However, I learnt more about Hugh Walpole, and at least discovered that he had this very admirable quality – the capacity to plod. Right at the beginning, apparently, Henry James had told him that if he went on, and on, and on, he would eventually get there. It seems to me that he *has* gone on, and on, and on, but that he has not got there. Still, the going is good.

Then I met him. The scene was Victoria Station on a raw morning in winter, with little wisps of yellow fog lurking under the high roof. The V.D.A.W. was ensconced in her carriage behind a large bouquet of roses which he had given to her. In her lap was an American magazine which he had also given her. I noticed with a slight amusement that it was 'featuring' a story by Hugh Walpole himself.

When the train bearing the V.D.A.W. had departed into the fog, we walked out of the station together.

'I hate seeing people off,' he said.

'So do I. Especially people I like.'

'Quite.'

He paused in the middle of the station and scratched his head.

'I should like to write a guide,' he said, 'on how to see people off. It would be done in several moods. Grave and gay. Topics to be avoided. Time-limits.'

'The chief thing,' I suggested, 'would be to strictly limit' (I noticed that the split infinitive made him blink, genteel man of letters that he was) 'to strictly limit the number of times one said, "Well, good-bye." We must have said it at least sixteen times this morning. Every whistle made us say it.'

'I don't remember saying it more than once,' he remarked.

Then we entered the Tube, and endeavoured to converse by shouting feverishly into each other's ears. (Oh! There is no doubt that we were meant to be enemies for life.)

'I hear you're doing dramatic criticism and book-reviewing,' he screamed.

'No, I'm not,' I bellowed. 'I'm only a reporter.' Bang, bang, bang.

'Well,' he shrieked, 'that's not as bad as the other.'

'What is not as bad as which?' I howled.

'I mean that book-reviewing' (and here the train suddenly came to a halt so that his voice boomed out like a sergeant-major's) 'is far more soul-destroying than reporting.'

I should like to see Hugh Walpole battering at East End doors on windy nights in winter, trying to gain admission to a house where a murder has just been committed, and see which he thought was more 'soul-destroying.'

'I did book-reviewing for a long time on the *Evening Standard*,' he confided, in a hoarse whisper, 'and' (here the train started, so he again had to yell) 'it nearly killed me.'

Bang, bang, bang.

'And what about the dramatic criticism?' I howled.

He gathered all the remaining wind that was in his lungs and shrieked, 'Don't know so much about it. But I should think that would rot your brain before long.'

He got out at Charing Cross, and as I hurtled along towards the unaristocratic destination of Blackfriars, I pondered on the type of mind that thought dramatic criticism would rot the brain. To see, night after night, the curtain rise on the flash and light of the drama. To feel, as every daylight faded, that some new pageant was gathering to spread itself out before one's eyes. To sit in the warm, scented darkness and analyse the motives, the construction, the technique of the play, even if it is a bad play. To have always the hope, sometimes justified, that one would be caught up in the sudden rapture that comes from great acting. Is that 'rotting the brain'? Not, I think, to a young man. However, Hugh Walpole is not a young man. He was born middle-aged. But he is rapidly achieving his first childhood.

CHAPTER TWENTY

A Memory – And Some Songs

ONE of the most wonderful evenings of my life was when, in the heart of the Australian Bush, Melba sang for me alone.

I ought, if I had a tidy mind, to describe how I got to the Australian Bush, and how so divine a person as Melba should be singing to me at all. But that can come in due course. For the moment I want to recapture that scene as I lived it.

There is a long room, panelled in green, lit only by the misty glow from outside the windows, fragrant with the scent of yellow roses. There are wonderful old mirrors that catch the dying sparkle of a Marie Antoinette chandelier. In the half-light so many lovely things shine dimly . . . a picture of dark, closely-clustered flowers, a case of fans, delicate as the world of fairies. . . .

I am standing at the window. There is a long veranda, and in the distance I can see, faintly out-lined, the pillars of the loggia that leads to an Italian garden. Mountains, fabulously blue, rise on the horizon and everything is very quiet. Only a few hours ago the air had been rent with the shrill cries of parrots, flying to their resting-place in the forests. Even while we had dined we could hear the liquid warbling of magpies, that strange noise, like water gurgling from a flask, which brings all Australia before me as I write. And after dinner, while we had taken our coffee, the whole of the fields around had echoed with the chirping of crickets. But now . . . silence.

And then, like a moonbeam stealing into an empty

room, that voice, which is as no other has ever been . . .

Dans ton cœur dort un clair de lune . . .

The notes die away and there is silence again. I go on looking at the blue mountains. Then, from the other end of the room, a sudden laugh, the sort of laugh that people may make in Heaven, and –

'Well, did you like me?'

I laugh too. It seems so utterly fantastic to attempt to appreciate in words an art like this. Nobody ought ever to clap Melba. They ought to remain silent. The greatest things in art are above applause.

It was in, I believe, 1923, that I first had the delight of meeting her, but it was not till the season had really begun, and I found myself in Covent Garden, listening to the first opening bars of '*Mi Chiamano Mimi*,' that I really came under her spell. It was not the first time I had heard her sing. As a small boy of nine I had been taken to one of her concerts by my mother, and had greatly irritated my family by informing them, when I returned home, that I thought she sang exactly like myself.

In a sense, there was truth as well as youthful complacency in that criticism. Her voice *is* like a choir-boy's, as crystalline, as utterly removed from things of the earth.

One day she said to me, with characteristic directness, 'You're not well. You're poisoned. You've been working too hard. You ought to come out to Australia and help me with my Opera Season.'

I denied indignantly that I was poisoned. (My doctor afterwards confirmed her diagnosis.) I said that

I knew nothing about Opera. But all the same, though it was some six months later, I went out to join her in Australia – that was in the beginning of 1924.

Melba is so great a woman – I use the word 'great' in the fullest sense – that one cannot possibly attempt a full-length portrait of her in a few pages. But, from the notebook of my imagination, I may perhaps draw out a few pages, roughly scribbled over with thumb-nail sketches, that may make you feel you know her a little.

I shall take the sketches simply as they occur, without attempting to put them in order. The first one is labelled 'energy.' The face of Melba appears, rising calmly over a heavy *chaise-longue* which, unassisted, she is pushing across the room. It is one of her furniture-moving days. The whole of her boudoir is upside down. Pictures stand in rows against the walls, china is ranged along the floor, and over the chairs and sofas are scattered quantities of bibelots – pieces of jade, little mother-of-pearl boxes bearing the words *Souvenir* and *Je pense à toi*, crystal clocks, a tiny gold case containing a singing bird with emerald eyes.

The furniture-moving goes on. I endeavour to help, and am told with great frankness that I am far more bother than I am worth, and that I had better content myself with watching. And so I watch, amazed. Little by little the room takes shape. At one moment she is standing on a chair, and the next she is kneeling on the floor, doing the work of six British labourers. *Voilà.* It is done. And she is at the piano again, trilling like a newly fed thrush.

If Melba had had no voice she might have made a fortune as an art connoisseur. I have been driving with her sometimes, and have seen, on the other side of the street, a window full of antiques. 'Look,' I have said. 'Don't you think there might be some fascinating things in there?' She looks. In the space of ten seconds her eye has taken in the entire contents of the window, and she either says 'All fake,' or she stops the car. I have never known her wrong. It is as inexplicable to me as the feat of the eagle which can see a mouse hidden in a field of corn a mile beneath.

So many people who like to pretend that they are artistic will tell you that they cannot bear to live with ugly things. They will say this with pained expressions, even when they are sitting, apparently unmoved, beneath a Landseer stag, on a Victorian settee. With Melba it really is pain. Whenever I see her in an ugly room I know the exact feeling of the Oyster who is irritated by a piece of sand. She is restless. Her eyes dart hither and thither. She bites her lips. For two pins she would get up and hurl things out of the window.

I shall never forget once when she was singing three times a week in the Opera at one of the great Australian cities, and was staying in an hotel in order to be near the theatre. She came down at about ten o'clock to go for a drive. I met her in the hall. As we were going out she paused in the entrance way and said: 'Those pots. Look at them. They're hideous enough in all conscience, but they're made ten times worse by being pushed out in that ridiculous position. Let's push them back against the wall.'

Now wherever Melba goes in Australia there is

always a little crowd in her wake, as though she were the Queen of the Continent, which indeed she is. And the prospect of moving pots in the entrance of an hotel struck me as alarming in the extreme.

I mumbled something about 'waiting.' She looked at me scornfully. 'Wait?' she said. 'What for? Come on.'

Without the faintest interest in the sensation she was making, she bent over and began to move the first pot into position. I shall never forget the sparkling look of satisfaction on her face, the slight flush that the effort caused, the waving ospreys in her hat, and the cry of 'There – isn't that better?' when the first pot was placed in position.

I saw a tall red-faced individual glowering down on us.

'Excuse me,' he said.

'I'm Melba,' she said. 'I'm doing some furniture-moving for you.'

He was quite speechless for a moment. Then, after a gulp he managed to say, 'But Madame . . .'

'Oh, I shan't charge you anything,' she remarked.

Those pots are as she placed them to this day.

The next sketch is labelled 'The Singing Lesson.' There are the outlines of a long bare room, a platform, some seats in front, occupied by professor and pupils. Melba sits by herself in a corner, biting a pencil. A pupil steps on to the platform and begins to sing. Suddenly the voice rings out, 'Stop!'

As though she had been shot, the pupil stops dead. Melba gets up from her seat, goes to the platform, says to the accompanist, 'Let me sit down a minute' and then turns to the girl.

'I'm not going to eat you, she says. Her own smile brings an answering smile to the face of the girl.

'Sing me "Ah." '

'Ah.'

'No – "Ah.' – up here, in the front of the mouth.'

'Ah!'

'No. You're still swallowing it. Listen. Sing mah. Close your lips, hum, and then open them suddenly. Mah, mah, mah.'

'Mah, mah, mah.'

'That's better. Now higher. Right. Higher.'

She takes her up the scale. At F sharp she stops. 'Piano. Please, please, *pianissimo!* You'll ruin your voice if you sing top notes so loud. Better, but still too loud. *Pianissimo!*' She leans forward, one finger to her lips.

Somewhere about the top B flat the girl cracks. She blushes and turns appealingly to Melba. Melba takes no notice and strikes a note higher.

'I don't think I can . . .'

'I don't care what you think,' says Melba. 'Sing it.'

'But I shall crack.'

'That doesn't matter, I don't mind what sort of noise you make. I just want to hear it.'

The girl attempts it again, the note is pure and round.

Melba rises from the piano and steps briskly from the platform. 'She's got a lovely voice,' she says. 'A lyric soprano. She's taking her chest notes too high, that's all. Send her up to me and I'll make that all right.'

I wonder how many other prima donnas there are in this world who would do that, who would put them-

206

selves to endless pains and expense, simply for the love of song.

I have yet to be informed of their names and addresses.

The third sketch is labelled – the artist. The scene is a rehearsal of *Othello*. For three hours she has been singing, directing, talking at one moment to the orchestra, at the next, to the stage hands, to anybody and everybody. The scene is set for the last act, and with her meticulous sense of detail she has been busying herself with the crimson draperies that over-hang the bed. Now she is standing in mid-stage, sending her voice up to the men who work the lights. 'More yellow,' she is crying, 'more yellow. This isn't a surgery. You're blinding me. That's better. Wait a minute. Not so much of that spot light on the bed. I am not a music-hall artist.' Then, *sotto voce*, 'How on earth does the poor man think that Desdemona could go to sleep with a light like that in her eyes?'

She is almost the only woman I have ever known who has an absolute horror of the slip-shod. Study her day when she is singing in opera. She is up with the lark. After breakfast she is in her boudoir, 'warming' her voice, studying her rôle from start to finish. She lunches frugally, drinking only water. After lunch she drives or walks. At five there is the pretence of a meal – an omelette or a little fish. From now onwards she eats nothing till after the perform-ance.

She is in her dressing-room from an hour and a half to two hours before the performance. Her make-up is scrupulous. She describes in her autobiography the importance which she attaches to the minutest details of make-up, but I don't think that even her own description quite makes one realize the perfection of it. From her wig to her shoes, everything is as it should be. I have seen her reject fifty shawls for the part of Mimi, simply because they were not in keeping with her idea of the character.

Sketch four might be named Courage. I remember a day when we were driving together, and, as she stepped from the car, the chauffeur slammed the door full on to her fingers, crushing them cruelly. She cried – 'Oh, my hand!' and the door was feverishly dragged open again. She bit her lip, walked into the theatre, sat down and closed her eyes. That was all. There was no hysterics, no 'Vapours,' not even a tear.

It is not only in physical courage that she excels. She has the sort of gay fearlessness which allows her to motor late at night through the Australian Bush with only a single chauffeur, and jewels of more value than I should care to estimate. One night she was motoring home with Lady Stradbroke, who is the wife of the Governor of Victoria. The car broke down in the middle of a forest. The chauffeur had to run off into the darkness, leaving the women alone. There they sat for a full hour. Any tramp, any of the roving, husky 'sun-downers' with whom the Bush abounds, might have come along and taken all they wanted. Lady Stradbroke told me that though she herself was shaking in her shoes, Melba kept up a perpetual babble of chatter. I asked her when at two o'clock in the morning they arrived, if she had not been fearfully agitated. She laughed her unforgettable laugh. 'Agitated? Me? They wouldn't hurt *me*. I'm Melba.'

'I'm Melba.' It is something to be able to say that. Something to be able to go up to an old woman selling roses in the streets of Paris and say '*C'est* Melba' and to have the roses pressed into your hands in a sort of homage. Something to know that wherever music is played or songs are sung all over the world, the artist who is playing before you is giving his utmost. Something to be able to lean back in the theatre stalls at a first night, and to say to Bernard Shaw, as I once observed, 'I know who *you* are' and to receive the answer: 'You don't know me nearly as well as I know you.'

And to remain, at the end of it all, so simple that you are never happier than when eating macaroni in a restaurant where you may have your fill for two shillings, so humble that you will kiss the cheek of the youngest débutante who, you feel, has in her something of the divine fire.

Melba, I salute you. It is not my fault that this sketch of you is so inadequate. It is yours. I cannot paint landscapes on threepenny bits.

CHAPTER TWENTY-ONE

Hicks – Hicks – and Nothing but Hicks

IT is a matter of very small importance either to
Seymour Hicks or to anybody else that I regard
him as capable of the finest acting on our stage. It
merely gives a keynote to what is written below, if
you should be kind enough to read it.

I never really knew Seymour until we went to
Australia on the same ship, and if you want to know
anybody well, go through that very disagreeable
experience, and nothing will be hidden from you. I
had of course met him in London, we had eaten
together, drunk together, and had feverish conversations in his dressing-room when he had arrived late
for his Act and was endeavouring to put on grease
paint at the rate of greased lightning.

But all that goes for nothing. Wait till you have
eaten stale fish and bottled cream at the same table
for six weeks, till you have been bitten by mosquitoes
at Colombo and rolled together in the Australian
Bight, till you have been bored silly by the ship's
wits and driven almost crazy by the ship's sopranos
– wait till you have done all those things, and somehow managed to come through them smiling, and
then you can certainly call a man a friend.

Admiration is never a bad basis on which to start a
friendship, and I passionately admired the artistry
of Seymour Hicks. Only recently I had seen his
performance in *The Love Habit*, and my eyes were
still dazzled by his performance. The accomplish-
ment of the man! The tricks! The diabolical clever-
ness! Watch him *listen*, for example. There is no
more difficult or less understood art on the stage than

this one of listening, and when you have seen Seymour listening, you have seen the whole thing,
inside-out, upside down, backwards. The head
slightly forward, the eyes fixed on the speaker, the
whole body set in a poise which seems to suggest a
question mark that gradually straightens itself out
as the question is resolved, to end as a mark of
exclamation. And the face! As each sentence is
uttered, he seems to hear it for the first time. A tiny
flicker at the mouth, a faint narrowing of the eyes,
an almost imperceptible wrinkling of the forehead
. . . if I were an actor I should go and hide my head
in shame after such an example of virtuosity.

And yet, with the exception of *The Man in Dress
Clothes*, things seem to have gone wrong with him
lately, while mediocre artists have made messes of
plays which he might have transfigured with his
genius.

One of the first things he ever told me was the truth
about *The Man in Dress Clothes* — the play which
was changed, in one night, from a failure to a success
owing to the intervention of Northcliffe.

'Funny thing, isn't it, what the Press can do for a
man?' he said to me one day. We were gliding
silently one evening down the long, straight reaches
of the Suez Canal, and the atmosphere of desert and
clean-washed sky seemed to lend itself to conversation. 'Take *The Man in Dress Clothes*, for example.
It had been running for three weeks when Northcliffe saw it, and up till then it had been an absolute
failure.'

'Why did Northcliffe come at all?' I asked.

'Max Pemberton. He told him about it, and Northcliffe wrote me a letter saying, "Dear Mr. Hicks, I don't usually like plays, but I will come to yours." He came to a matinée. After the first Act he sent a special messenger down to Carmelite House to order some of his staff up to the theatre at once, and when I went to see him after the second Act he said to me:

"'These gentlemen have just been instructed to bo om your play, Mr. Hicks. It's the best play I've ever seen. There will be a photograph of it in every edition of the *Daily Mail* for the next month, and a paragraph in the *Evening News* telling London that London has got to come and see it.'"

'And, by Jove, they did come to see it. On the next day, in the *Evening News* appeared an article about my play headed "The best play in London," and the same night the receipts were multiplied five times over. It became almost embarrassing. I used to get almost afraid of opening the Northcliffe papers to see what they had written next. All the same, it kept that play running for a year, and I am eternally grateful to Northcliffe for that.'

One of the most interesting conversations I ever had with him was, of all places, at the Sydney Zoo. Not that the Sydney Zoo is like ordinary zoos. It is very superior, in fact almost beautiful. It lies above the eternal blue of Sydney harbour, looking over the waves to where the white houses and red roofs glitter in the sunshine. There are wattle trees to give you a touch of yellow (how I wish Australians would call wattle by its proper name – mimosa) and there are flame trees to give you a touch of scarlet. And the animals in this particular zoo do not seem to be in the zoo at all, for there are not cages, but pits. So that there is a fine thrill waiting for anybody who does not know this, for all the animals look as though they are about to leap out to devour.

The zoo had nothing to do with our conversation, but I cannot dissociate it from its surroundings. Seymour was standing in front of a paddock containing a number of kangaroos, which leapt about, disdainfully regarding the stale monkey-nuts which were thrown to them by sticky children. The kangaroo does not eat stale monkey-nuts. I have no idea what he does eat, but he does not eat that.

He gazed absently at the kangaroo for a moment, threw it a peppermint drop, and said:

'Of course the only critic who's going to be of any use to the English Theatre to-day is the man who talks about the *acting*.'

'You mean the acting before the play?' I said. 'I love talking to you, because you agree with everything I say. You may say that the star system is overdone, but no star, if he *was* a star, has ever done anything but good to the theatre. He ennobles everything he touches.'

Seymour nodded. 'Look at Edmund Kean. Columns and columns of Press cuttings I've got about him. They really criticized in those days. They watched every movement, every gesture, they listened to every intonation of the voice. They put him through a third degree of criticism.'

'And he came out triumphant?'

'Not always. Pretty often. Anyway, what I mean is, they concentrated on the *acting*, and they set tremendously high standards. Look at half the critics to-day. They don't care a damn. They spend half their time in an analysis of the play itself, which interests nobody, and then they say that somebody or other was "brilliant." It's wrong. A critic ought to have two ink-pots, vitriol and gold. And he ought to be jolly sparing with the gold one.'

'The very first thing that struck me about the theatre,' I said (I wanted, you see, to encourage him to talk), 'when I began criticism, was that we were too afraid of being theatrical. Now, I like a theatre to look like a theatre, to smell like a theatre, to feel like a theatre. I don't like a theatre that looks like a church or a town hall. I like . . .'

This conversation is beginning to sound like a dialogue in the deceased *Pall Mall Gazette*, but I really don't mind. Seymour agreed with me, and said:

'I'd far rather see somebody come on and say, "Gadsooks. My mistress has forsaken me," and say it as though he meant it, than see a young man in a beautiful dinner-jacket light a cigarette, and mumble, "Oh really, Flora seems to have gone off with Rupert" as though he were saying, "It's a rather cold morning, isn't it?" The last thing an actor should fear is to be thought theatrical. When a really good actor of the old school came on he struck an attitude. He bounced. He filled the stage. You said, "By God, here's an actor," and you jolly well watched what he did. Irving for example.

'Irving realized the enormous importance of a first entrance. Look at his King Lear. Heralds approach. A train of soldiers. More heralds. The suspense increasing every moment. You can almost feel him coming. You lean forward in your seat, awake, ex-

pectant. And then – enter Irving, slowly, with a
falcon on his wrist. Now that's *acting*. That isn't any
nonsense about being life-like or trying to look as
though you weren't an actor. As soon as a man does
that, he *doesn't* look like an actor, because he isn't
one, and never will be, and his place is in the thirtieth
row of a cinema, watching glycerine run down Mary
Pickford's cheeks.'

There is more sound sense – I *could* call it profound
wisdom, but I won't – in those remarks than in half
the nonsense that is written to-day about 'realistic'
plays and 'realistic' acting. You might as well talk
about 'realistic' music and praise a composer who sits
down at the piano and tries to imitate a waterfall.

One night I was dining with Ellaline Terris and him,
and it suddenly occurred to me to tell them the plot
of a rather gruesome short story which had come
into my head a few days before. When I had finished
Seymour said, 'My word, what a play!' In fact,
everybody said, 'My word, what a play!' And there
and then we hunched ourselves round the table and
began to talk it out.

Of course, we never did talk it out. That is why it
is so charming a memory. But Seymour can teach
one more about play-making in a few hours than
most of the books (or, indeed, the plays) in the world.
And people seem to be interested in play-making.
They like to know 'how it is done.' So here goes.

The first thing that he talked about was the absolute necessity of deciding exactly who the characters
were. It sounds obvious enough, but if you have
ever thought of writing a play you will probably
remember that you thought of a woman in a certain

situation, and beyond the fact that you knew she was good, bad, or merely improper, you did not know the first thing about her.

But, before we decided on a single line, we had to make those people real people. We had to know not only what their lives were, but what they had been, and why. In other words, we had to delve deep back into the past (long before the period of my short story), into the drama of the past, in order that we might approach the drama of the present with minds forewarned.

And then, when we had decided who the people were, we had to decide exactly what the story was. All this sounds fantastically obvious, but I assure you, it is not so obvious as it sounds. Take again your own case, if you are an amateur playwright, as I feel convinced you are, you have probably thought of it all in *Acts*. You have said the first Act will be set in an attic, and will end with the arrest of Joseph on a charge of some vice – (naming your own favourite one). The second Act will be in a ball-room, in which Joseph's fiancée will spurn the Duke. And the third Act will be in a court of justice, where Joseph is declared innocent. It is all wrong. You mustn't do that. You mustn't even think of the theatre at all. You must think of life, of what is happening to these people in the open air, in bed, when they are asleep, when they are in their baths. Think of them as real human beings. And then, when you have decided what they are doing, what they have done, and what they are going to do, then go at it for all you're worth, and be as theatrical as a Christmas fairy, and good luck to you.

And the other thing I learnt during those hours after midnight in which we sat conspiring together, was that not a line must be written before the construction is absolutely water-tight. You have to build a play – a good play – like a jigsaw puzzle. Every little bit must fit. There must be so much this, and so much that. There must be a place for everything, and everything in its place. If you dribble into dialogue too soon, you are done. God help you, for you will be like a ship without a rudder, and you will lose your way in a sea of talk, blown by the winds of every passing mood.

It sounds prosaic. There is nothing of the thrill, which comes to those who dash to their tables at midnight, and write out passionate speeches in which perfect ladies declare their innocence and imperfect women their guilt. But, after all, the greatest fun, I should think, is seeing your play *played*. And the impromptu, passionate sort of play doesn't usually get beyond the paper on which it is scrawled.

CHAPTER TWENTY-TWO

Showing how a Genius worshipped Devils in the Mountains

ALL young men love paying pilgrimages, especially when the pilgrimage is to some rather exotic and remote hermit who happens to be in the vogue. Incidentally, I am quite convinced that the hermits like it too. How often has one read, in memoirs, of the humble, too humble, delight of some wild musician who is visited, in his retreat in the Northern Hebrides, by young things from Oxford, who group themselves in decorative attitudes round his carpet slippers. 'To me, living in the realm of art,' he writes, 'these visits from fellow-spirits in the outer world are infinitely sweet, infinitely welcome. Mr. Bernard Bank, of Brasenose, arrived to-day at dawn, praying that I might come down, so that he should throw himself at my feet. I did. And he did. I feel "remarkably refreshed."'

I rather wish that I had gone to see Norman Lindsay in this way. He has all the qualifications for a really good hermit scene. He lives in the heart of the Blue Mountains beyond Sydney, he is an utterly isolated figure in an immense continent, and his finely erotic designs have given a great many dull people fits.

But my visit to him, though picturesque, was sophisticated. I went out to see him with Melba in an exceedingly comfortable car, and after three hours of speeding along under tall white gum-trees, with the flash of green parrots in the branches, we arrived at the broken, tumble-down road which leads to the house where Norman Lindsay lives with his wife and children.

The instant I had passed through the wooden gate, which was blistered by the eternal blaze of sunshine, I had a feeling of stepping on to enchanted ground. (You observe, the hermit complex was already at work.) From some bushes over in the corner a fawn's head leered at me through the shadows, and on the grass leading up to the house a concrete lady with an enormous chest stared haughtily in front of her. Advancing to the veranda one had a glimpse of the same lady, flying in haste from presumably the same fawn — a really beautiful piece of rough statuary which Lindsay afterwards informed me had been roughly 'thrown together' in the space of a single afternoon.

As for Lindsay himself — he did not walk towards us — he fluttered to us, like a bird. So like a bird is he that I had a feeling, all the time, that I must catch hold of the end of his jacket in order that he should not fly up to a gum-tree and pipe his distracting arguments from the topmost branch. He was so thin, so fluttering, his eyes were so bright, his nose so like a beak, perched on top of the tiny neck.

As for his talk — that, too, was bird-like — the words pouring out one after the other, making one think of when the swallows homeward fly. As difficult to follow, too, as a bird. In the first half-hour of our conversation — (I say 'our,' although my contribution was limited to negatives and affirmatives) — he had smashed the whole Christian philosophy, set Nietzsche on a pedestal, made at least a hundred genuflexions to him, pulled a long nose at Rubens, kicked Chopin out of the house, and invited me three times to have a drink without doing anything more about it.

We went for a walk in the garden, Lindsay still talking. A child appeared — a rosy-cheeked thing with cherries embroidered round its collar. It was clasping a doll firmly in its arms.

'The maternal instinct developed already, you see,' he said.

Odd, I thought. I felt that Freud had dropped something which Lindsay had picked up, taken to a looking-glass, and read backwards.

Somebody again suggested a glass of white wine. This time his eyes sparkled. We went back into the house and drank. I watched him. He talked of the wine as though he were a Bacchanalian. One had the impression that he was only five minutes off a bout of drunkenness. Yet, he sipped only a mouthful, and even that was taken with pursed lips, as an old lady takes her tea.

Odd, again. It was the *idea* of intoxication, you see, that appealed to him. The gesture was the important thing, not the reality. I honestly believe that Lindsay could get quite drunk on coloured water, if he were persuaded the water was wine.

And then we went into lunch. I remember a room with huge windows and sunshine blazing in. I remember an enormous plate of chicken and some very red carrots. And most of all I remember Lindsay's sudden pæon of praise in favour of Beethoven's Appassionata Sonata.

'He's my god,' he said excitedly, digging his fork into a particularly beautiful carrot and waving it wildly about. 'My god. The Appassionata Sonata contains everything of life that life has to give. In its rhythm you can find the secret of the entire universe.' He ran from the room and returned bearing a mask of Beethoven which he triumphantly placed beside him.

I cannot give you much of Norman Lindsay's talk because I simply did not understand it. He talks at such an immense speed, dragging so many tattered philosophies in his wake, that one could only follow, exceedingly faint, but pursuing.

However, I did not give up the attempt. I tried to keep him strictly to facts, and after lunch I led him to one of his concrete ladies and asked him how he did it.

His thin hand stroked the concrete lady's chin with a lingering affection. But he took not the faintest notice of my question, and started off on a different tack.

'There are only two people whom I want to meet in England,' he said. 'I wonder if you can guess who they are?'

Now, I never guess when asked. It is too dangerous. Do you know the sort of people who have a face massage, arrange the lights, hold their chins very high, and say 'you won't guess *my* age, I'm sure.' They are quite right. I won't.

Norman Lindsay relieved the suspense. 'Aldous Huxley and Dennis Bradley,' he said.

'*What?*'

There must have been something a little tactless in my tone of voice, for he frowned and said, 'Well, I don't see why you should be so surprised.'

I was surprised, however, because it seemed such

an odd couple to choose. Lytton Strachey I could have imagined. Shaw, at a pinch. Augustus John more than most. But Aldous Huxley and Dennis Bradley . . .

I still do not know, from the whirl of words with which he defended his two idols, exactly what he meant. But from out of the chaos there did eventually emerge something — that he considered them both anti-Christian. Perhaps, after the psychic experiments of Dennis Bradley, his ardour may have abated. I don't know.

Lindsay hates Christ. He hates him as one man hates another. It is in no way the feeble sort of dislike which so many modern anti-Christians entertain — the dislike which is explained merely by the fact that Christ makes them feel uncomfortable, as though he were a skeleton at the feast of life. It is a militant, violent hatred, the clash of one philosophy against another. He ranges himself, a solitary figure, against the angels, his whole mind and body tense with rage, his hand gripped grimly round an unsheathed sword.

It was not till I went with him to his studio, which is a sort of wooden shack at the end of the garden, that I began to understand this dislike. He danced round with portfolio after portfolio, producing drawings which were a riot of pagan beauty, a miracle of design. But the beauty and the art he seemed to pass by. It was the satire — the anti-Christian satire — which he was longing to show me.

'Look,' he said. I looked. He was holding up an immense engraving crowded with figures. I have a dim memory of light shining through pillars, of an endless staircase, of a conglomeration of strange, dishevelled shapes, darkly etched in the foreground.

'Amazing,' I said.

'Yes – yes – but don't you see him?'

'Him?'

'Jesus Christ, man. Look.'

He put his finger on to the design. It touched a pale face – sickly, anæmic, almost half-witted. It was like a patch of fever in the riotous health and brutality which crowded it in on all sides.

He laughed loud and long. I could not laugh. I felt absurdly, desolatingly shocked. Not, I think, by what Lindsay had shown me of Christ. But by something which he had shown me of – myself.

CHAPTER TWENTY-THREE

A Defence of Dramatic Critics

A LITTLE while ago Mr. Philip Guedalla (that squib who never stops fizzing) annoyed me very much by making rude remarks about dramatic critics. He said that they looked like waiters or conjurers. I should not in the least mind looking like some waiters I have seen, but he was not referring to face or figure. He was being sartorial. And when Guedalla is sartorial, God alone knows what will happen.

He referred to the 'dingy uniform' of this 'Sad Guild.' It struck me as slightly vulgar and entirely inaccurate. I would match my own exquisite waistcoats (you know the sort – nothing at the back and a broad pique in front) with Mr. Guedalla's any day. It would be rather an entertaining match. I can imagine our respective laundresses panting for days beforehand, and I can see us strutting round and round, examining each other for the faintest sign of a wrinkle.

But it is not of clothes that I would write, but of dramatic criticism, and the only excuse I have for holding up an imaginary Guedalla by the scruff of his neck is because of that phrase 'Sad Guild.' It is a childish, facile, meaningless phrase. It calls up the stale conventional vision of rows of gloomy faces, 'like Micawbers waiting for something to turn down.' It is the sort of phrase that an unsuccessful playwright might use, to excuse his failure. As if critics, by some Satanic grace, were gifted with power to fool *all* the public, in *all* the theatres, *all* the time.

I am a dramatic critic. I know of no sad guild. I

have yet to wear a dingy uniform. Every time that I go to a theatre it is with a heart beating high in hope. Every time that I open a programme and read that 'the curtain will be lowered for thirty seconds in Act II to denote the passing of a hundred years,' I tremble with the satisfaction that only make-believe can give. Every time I read that Mr. Clarkson has sold a few more wigs, my being trembles with delight. To be a dramatic critic does not imply that one must be old and shrivelled and pessimistic.

I was absurdly young when I began. And I didn't care a damn. If love of the theatre was any qualification for criticism, then I was qualified with the highest degrees. My first toy was a toy theatre. In the misty days of the late King Edward VII I have lain for whole seasons on my small stomach putting pink heroines and black villains in their proper places. I have burnt candles for footlights as ardently as any human saint burnt candles for sacrifice. I have drawn thunder from a tin can and lightning from a piece of tinsel. And at school, when I should have been engaged on more orthodox matters, I have routed out ancient books on the theatre – as Æchylus knew it in Greece, as Goldoni knew it in Italy, and, in dreams, have fought my youthful battles on those vanished stages, made mock love with adolescent passion, closed my eyes, and been, in rapid succession, hero, heroine, cynic, clown, every emotion tearing my young heart to tatters.

If you please, therefore, Mr. Guedalla, protrude your pink tongue, apply your blue pencil to it, and erase that phrase about the sad guild in its dingy uniform. It is unworthy of you, for you can fizz very prettily, at times.

I forget the name of the first play which I was ever called upon to criticize, except that it was a worthless 'comedy' in the West End by somebody who was evidently not fit to produce even a one-act sketch. But with what infinite conscientiousness I attacked my task! I went armed with two pencils, one of which I produced from time to time in order to scribble furtively on the back of the programme, trying not to be seen and yet half hoping that somebody would see me, and realize that I really was a dramatic critic. However, it was exceedingly difficult to work under such conditions. One had rather to bend down and crumple one's waistcoat (which would bring one perilously near the condition of 'sad uniform'), or else content oneself with a few desultory scrawls which were usually illegible at the end of the performance.

From such scraps, at first, was the criticism written, late at night, while the echo of the drama still seemed to hover in the air. But after a time I learnt that far the best criticisms were written entirely from memory, at least a day after the play. Sometimes, if there was a première on the night in which we were going to press, it would be necessary to dash into the office and write half a column in twenty minutes, surrounded by the buzz and clash of great machines printing late editions. But criticizing in those circumstances was dangerous — very dangerous. So elating, so intoxicating is the atmosphere of the theatre, that a good actress seems transfigured, for the moment, into a great genius. Not until the morning comes do we realize only too often that she is just – good.

For every capable play I saw – not great, but well-constructed and interesting – I must have seen, at a very charitable estimate, twenty bad ones. A mysterious thing the theatre. Entirely incalculable one would imagine, for the average run of men. I have asked myself time and again, during the last year or so, by what dark process certain plays have ever been born at all. I have sat back in my stall, in wide-eyed innocence, listening to the sort of dialogue that, one imagines, takes place during the meat-teas of our lesser lunatic asylums, endeavouring to be interested in situations that contain nothing new, nothing dramatic, nothing vital in any way whatever. And I say why? Why?

I ask myself the same question during the *entr'acte* in the bar, with its warm humanity, its grotesque barmaids, its sparkling taps and glasses. Here, where life is throbbing and intense, where the presumably evil passions of those who have not drunk are offset by the soft desires of those who have, the drama which one has just been observing seems infinitely petty – the *dramatis personæ* as ghosts blown willy-nilly across a desolate stage by the winds of nonsense. Again I wonder why?

Before I endeavour to answer that question let me say that when I see a real play I do not go to the bar. I either remain attached to my seat in a state of trance, or else I go out by myself into the street, collide violently with the stomachs of large fat men, get splashed by motor-buses, and creep back, like a worshipper, just as the lights are being turned down.

We have still not answered the question, Why do such bad plays get produced at all? The chief reason, I believe, is that one of the most important people in the theatre is still paid rather less than the ladies who sweep the carpets. That person is the play-reader. Mr. Edward Knoblock was a play-reader before he wrote *Kismet*, and told me that he used to read something like three thousand plays a year, working all day and a good deal of the night, for some fantastically small sum, like two pounds a week. Yet, on his decision (and very often on his extra work in re-writing them), depended the expenditure of thousands of pounds, and the making or losing of a small fortune.

We have recently had a very illuminating illustration of the mentality of the play-reader. A woman who for twenty years has been reading plays for London managers (who, presumably, have been guided by her advice), suddenly wrote a play herself, in collaboration with a man whose name I forget.

The play was duly produced, and it ran, by a miracle, for a week. It was a farce, in both senses of the word. No adjective in any language can describe its dreariness. (I believe there is a word in Russian, which deals with a particular mental disease known only among grave-diggers, but I have forgotten it.) If a nonconformist father and a Baptist mother had produced a daughter of the lowest intelligence, who had sedulously been kept from entering the theatre until she was thirty, at which date she had been to a pierrot performance on a small sea-side pier on a rainy day at the end of the season, and had then returned with a splitting headache to record her impressions, that was the sort of play she would write. Ten sentences of it, in typescript, would have given the average reader a feeling of desolate despair that the human brain could conceive such banalities.

And yet, the author, for twenty years, has been (and to the best of my knowledge, still is) a form of despot before whom all aspiring young playwriters must make obeisance. She is the gate through which they must pass, the play-doctor who must pronounce them sound. It is all wrong. She may be a good mother, a brave woman, with a positive passion for dumb animals. But she never has, never will, and never can, be qualified to judge of any matter even remotely connected with the theatre.

With one notable exception – I need not name him – we know practically nothing about 'scene' in the sense that Mr. Gordon Craig uses the word. We use a lighting system as casually as we switch on a light in our own bathrooms. We stick chairs higgledy-piggledy all over the room, not realizing that in a play a chair is a perpetual *note*, a monotone perhaps, but still playing its part in the general harmony or discord. We have had one or two attempts at significant scenery in England lately, but the scenery was so significant that it entirely dwarfed the actors, who themselves were none too strong that they should be robbed of even a little of their personality. One had a sense of infinite sideboards, one was caught in the rapture that belongs to a really seductive sofa. And the play went to pot.

It has needed an American to show us what scenery

can be. Need I say that I refer to Mr. Robert Jones's designs for John Barrymore's production of *Hamlet*? It is the most superb scenery I have seen in any part of the world – the soaring arch, lost in gloom, brooding, sometimes outlined in a sudden fretted splendour, tremendously aloof, like the gesture of some genius who alone fully comprehended the recessed mysteries of Hamlet's soul. If I know the smallest thing about the theatre, that was great scenery – as great, in its way, as the play itself.

Writing of Robert Jones – who, as one of the most important men in the modern theatre, ought to be as well known in this country as Bernard Shaw is in America – makes me want to 'have you meet him,' because hardly anybody over here seems even to have heard of him at all. He is exquisitely erratic. I have spoken of the marvellous arch which he made for *Hamlet*, but I did not betray the secret of its inspiration. That came from Mont St. Michel. And this was Robert Jones's method of getting to Mont St. Michel.

He was going to Paris with an old friend. By some strange freak they entered a train which was continually stopping at stations. After an hour or so it stopped at a tiny station, surrounded by fields of blue flowers, with hills beckoning in the distance.

'Let's get out,' said Robert.

'Let's,' replied the friend, who, with geniuses, always acquiesced.

They got out, seized their luggage. Outside was an old Ford car. The luggage was placed upon it.

Robert took out a map. 'It is only a few hundred miles from here,' he said, 'to the sea. If we go straight across country we shall reach Mont St. Michel.' He made a rapid calculation. 'We should arrive at dawn. The towers will be rising out of the mist.' (To the coachman) – 'Drive to Mont St. Michel.'

And by that fiery spirit was created the scene which, to me, is the only setting worthy of *Hamlet*.

It would be interesting to know the extent to which the censor has contributed to the present state of affairs. I think he is more objectionable as a distasteful symbol than as a functioning official. The obvious and natural idea that censorship in any form whatever is more immoral than the most indecent work that can come from a human brain has not yet penetrated our still medieval intelligences, but it is gradually becoming evident.

Professor A. M. Low, that brilliant young inventor, once said to me that in a few hundred years an umbrella will seem as monstrously absurd to our descendants as witch-burning seems to-day. The idea of censorship will, I believe, share the fate of the umbrella. If a dramatist wishes to express an idea by filling his stage with naked and debased creatures, it seems to me amazing that anybody should have the impudence to stop him. You are not forced into a theatre, any more than you are forced to observe the antics of dogs in the streets. You can stay away. You can . . . .

But there. This is not 2125. It is 1925. One must wait – like the witches.

CHAPTER TWENTY-FOUR

In which William Somerset Maugham makes a Delicate Grimace

WILLIAM SOMERSET MAUGHAM has no public personality. Although *Lady Frederick* has been prancing about the stages of the world for nearly twenty years — dear thing — although the 'leaves' still 'tremble,' and although 'Rain' is apparently never going to cease showering golden drops into the pocket of its creator, William Somerset Maugham remains William Somerset Maugham. He does not, like other successful authors, suddenly develop piercing eyes, or a villa in Capri, or a pony, or a rose garden, or any of the usual accompaniments of fame.

Why there are so few tales about him, I can't imagine, for his life abounds in the sort of 'copy' which would bring a flush to the cheeks of even the weariest Press agent. The story of his early struggles, for example. He told it to me on one evening full of hope, when the first adolescent strawberries had been discovered in the Café Royal, and were blushing at the last oysters, the like of which they would never see again, it being the last of April's days.

I can see him now, one cheek pink by the light of the red lamp by his side, the other pale by the light of nature. His black eyes sparkled like sloes dipped in wine, and, had a hundred others not forestalled me, I should have said that 'the eyelids were a little weary, as though this were the head upon which all the ends of the world were come.' Maugham's eyelids always are a little weary, but his mouth is invariably on the verge of a smile.

'When I came to London,' he said, 'I had £3,000. I was twenty years old, and I made up my mind that I should write for a living. For ten years I wrote, but I hardly lived. Nobody would put on my plays, and though my novels were published, nobody appeared anxious to read them.

'When I was thirty I had reached my last hundred pounds. I was mildly desperate. And then, somebody suddenly decided, in a moment of aberration, that they would produce a play of mine. The play was *Lady Frederick*.

'I knew that if *Lady Frederick* was a failure I should have to give up the idea of writing any more, and should spend the rest of my days in an office. I had no particular hope that it would be anything but a failure, especially as the producer came to me, a few days before the first night, and told me that there weren't enough epigrams. "We want at least two dozen more epigrams," he said. I blinked at him, went away to have a cup of tea, and put in the epigrams with a trembling hand, rather as though I were a new cook sticking almonds on to the top of her first cake.

'Well, I arrived at the theatre on the first night, knowing that I should leave it either as an accomplished dramatist or an embryo bank clerk. I left it as the former. I knew, from the very beginning that the play was a success, because they began to laugh almost as soon as the curtain had risen. I think it's a great thing to get a laugh in one's first few lines.'

The adjective which is always used as a sort of sign-post when Maugham is under discussion is the one word in the English language which I thoroughly detest. I mean, of course, 'cynical.' It is the sort of word that is used by speckled young women at tennis parties, when one attempts to vary the monotony of the game by making a few gentle reflections to one's partner on the futility of existence. I once met somebody (this is terrible, but true), who said to me the meaningless, damning words, 'I'm an awful cynic, you know.' That person went to prison. I understand the warders were so kind to him that he is now a raving sentimentalist.

We will, therefore, if you please, rule out this epicene adjective from our discussion of William Somerset Maugham. Let us say, rather, that he has the honesty to admit that he finds life quite meaningless, seeing it merely as a procession of grotesque, painted figures winding out of the darkness into a momentary patch of light, and then drifting into a deeper darkness still. But he does not beat his breast, in the manner of Thomas Hardy, and rend the clouds over Bryanston Square with blasphemies. He lies back, lights a cigarette, beckons to a few of the more ridiculous persons in the procession, and sets them dancing on the stage of his own imagination. And I can quite believe that the substantial royalties which result are far more satisfactory than any misty philosophies.

I am not speaking without the book. He summed it all up once by saying to me, 'I think that life has a great deal of rhyme and absolutely no reason. I entirely fail to see that it means anything whatever. It justifies itself only by the amusement it gives one.'

The occasion on which these bold and bad words

issued from his lips was, if I remember rightly, at a party where he, in the velvet smoking-jacket which he wears on all possible occasions, was lying gracefully against the back of a sofa. H. G. Wells was sitting bolt upright in an arm-chair, while I sat most appropriately on the floor. Thus I was at the feet of two masters at the same time. A sensation which, had I been an American tourist, would probably have resulted in apoplexy. H. G. Wells had admitted to a completely open mind on the whole problem of existence, which, I presume, was the cause of Maugham's confession.

But I don't wish to give the impression that he strikes one merely as a facile, elegant figure, skating on the surface of things, cutting arabesques on the ice. His polished agnosticism is the result of a deeper thought than the hearty optimism of many tiresome philosophers. He told me once of the lasting emotion he experienced when, in a remote cave in Java, he discovered frescoes, a thousand years old, of peasants, using almost precisely the same instruments as were used in the fields of Devonshire and Cornwall to-day.

For a moment he looked entirely serious. 'It gave me an overwhelming realization of the changelessness of man,' he said. 'It wasn't so much the fact that they were using the same sorts of spades and hoes. One saw beyond that into the essential sameness of their personalities. Nothing is ever altered.' And then the smile came back again. 'I can't make out whether it depresses me or not.'

His style, in the same way, is no airy stringing of words, no naïve and unstudied grouping of language. Like his philosophy, it has emerged from many experiments. 'I think I have at last got down to the bare bones of style,' he said. 'I try to say what I have to say with the greatest possible economy of language. I used to be terribly elaborate and ornate. Now I write as though I were writing telegrams. And when I have finished, I go over it all again to see what can be deleted.'

Maugham, I think, is eternally surprised that people find him shocking. It *is* odd, but not so odd as the fact that *The Circle* (which was regarded in London as so innocent that hardly a single bishop fell out of his pulpit about it) was found so hideously immoral in Paris that the great majority of managers refused to take the responsibility of putting it on. I was even more amazed when he told me that *Lady Frederick*, which the Edwardians so genteelly applauded, caused a great many heads to be shaken in Germany, and apparently provided the Teutonic race with an excellent proof of the decadence of English society.

Speaking of the translations of his plays reminds me of a good story. I once asked him what sort of sensation one had when one heard one's work played in a foreign language; if it made the author's breast swell with pride, or if it was merely irritating.

'I once found myself in Petrograd,' he said, 'and I was excessively bored. I hardly understood Russian at all, but I decided that the only way in which to cheer myself up was to go to the theatre. I went to the theatre, choosing the largest and cleanest-looking one I could find, and sat down to watch the play.

'It was a comedy, and, as far as one could judge, the audience seemed to find it amusing. It did not amuse me in the least, because I couldn't understand a single word of what it was about. But towards the end of the first Act it seemed to me that there was something vaguely familiar about the situation on the stage. I had a sense of listening to something I had heard in a dream. I looked down at the programme to discover who had written it. The author's name was Mum. And the name of the play was *Jack Straw*.'

It was at Wembley, strangely enough, that he made the most provocative statement which I have ever heard him make – the sort of statement which sticks uncomfortably in one's mind, like a burr. It was really my fault, because Wembley, as usual, had depressed me to distraction. To wander through halls of bottled gooseberries, called 'Canada,' and bottled peaches, called 'Australia'; to drag one's feet past hideous engines, labelled 'Industry,' and to listen to the indecent shrieks of young women on toboggans, called 'Amusement,' strikes me as one of the grimmest jests which life has to offer.

There was only one thing to do in this sort of environment, and that was, to talk about love. To talk at it, rather. I began to mutter platitudes about love being a condition impossible of attainment, an alchemy that had never been discovered. That no two people ever loved each other with an equal fire. That the only possible love implied the most rigid and exacting fidelity, in thought as well as in deed. And that nobody (except bores and half-wits) ever achieved this condition.

Then suddenly Maugham cut through these gloomy clouds with one shattering sentence. '*I don't see why one shouldn't love people flippantly,*' he said.

'Flippantly!'

There danced before my eyes the ghosts of light ladies on broad terraces, terraces which only knew the moonlight and were always mysterious with the heady scent of dark roses. Flippantly! So many difficulties solved, so many problems blown, like a puff of smoke, over the thick forest in which I was wandering. If only one could recapture the age in which those remarks really expressed a mode of life. Here, in the British Empire Exhibition, the idea of 'loving anybody flippantly' sounded almost like treason, as though one had stolen into the Australian pavilion by night, and had extracted one of the bottled gooseberries to see if they really tasted as nasty as they looked.

And yet, I believe it is the right attitude. — No, I don't. I believe it is the most comfortable attitude. It is neither right nor wrong, it is simply a matter of temperament. If, however, there were a little more flippancy in the world, there might be a few less wars. Swords cannot be unsheathed flippantly. Poison cannot be made with an airy gesture. Notes cannot be flicked across the Channel from one ambassador to another, like blowing kisses. If they could, they might not cause so much trouble.

That is, I think, the tremendously important function that Maugham plays in the world to-day. He says to the world, 'I know no more about things than you. I have not the faintest idea where I came

238

from, whither I am going. Yes, I quite agree that we are in a very distressful condition. But, just a moment . . .' (and here he takes one by the arm), 'if you look over in that direction, you will see a man with an extraordinarily amusing face. He is talking to a woman who is pretending to be in love with him. How tragic? Not in the least. If you only realized, it is exceptionally amusing. Now listen, and I will tell you a story. . . .'

CHAPTER TWENTY-FIVE

In which Michael Arlen Disdains Pink Chestnuts

IN 1870, had you chanced to be walking over one of the rough and alarming roads that stretched across the Balkans, from Roustchouk to Constantinople, you might have met a young man driving a bullock cart. He would have been tall and dark, with a certain weariness round his black eyes, and what might be described as 'a grim determination' round his lips. (Yes – we will get to Michael Arlen in a moment.)

The young man was setting out to make his fortune. And he made it. Not all at once, it is true, for the road from Roustchouk to Constantinople is long, and, I should imagine, in 1870 it was even longer. And one cannot make a great fortune quickly when one has only £20 with which to buy Turkish delights, even when one sells them at double the money. Bandits, too, who emerged from the forlorn countryside and attacked one in the rear, were apt to make great inroads into one's fortune. However, in time, the young man had saved £50, at the age of 19. (Yes, Michael Arlen is getting nearer and nearer.)

When the young man had made his £50 he bought a beautiful coat of blue velvet, with a scarf of coloured wool, and he was the beau of the village. All the Armenian girls cast their black eyes in his direction. His weariness, in consequence, was slightly alleviated. (I can hear Michael Arlen chafing in the next paragraph.)

One Sunday, this fine young man put on his velvet suit and went for a drive round the town in

an open cab. Apart from the open cab, it was perhaps the greatest day in his life. For as he was
passing under a certain high window, he looked up
and saw a girl who was fairer than any girl he had
ever seen. Their eyes met, and they were in love.
She drew back from the window, and cried, as all
true lovers should. He frowned, told the cab to
drive him home, and went in his blue velvet coat to
demand her hand from her father. And as soon as
her father had said 'yes,' the first line, one might
say, was written of *The Green Hat*. For the young
man was Michael Arlen's father.

I have introduced Michael Arlen in this manner
because it seems in some way to heighten the
romance of his career. They had a great deal in
common, his father and he. They both treated life
as an adventure, and doing so, gained a rich reward.
The only difference being that Arlen senior went
into business, whereas Arlen junior kept out of it.
Arlen senior lost his money in the war. Arlen junior
made his money in the peace.

A very dainty young man I thought him, when we
first drank wine together at an hour when the last
silk hat has drifted shamelessly home in the Mayfair
dawn — (which is as no other dawn). I use the word
'dainty,' not to indicate effeminacy, but to convey a
certain nicety of manner, a delicacy of tact. A very
charming young man, it seemed, after the third
glass of wine. A very brilliant young man, I was
convinced, after the sixth. And I keep to the latter
opinion, now that I am sober.

So few people know him. He has such a tiresome
legend attached to him – a gilt-edged legend. He

has been dehumanized in the popular imagination by his success. I hate writing biographies of anybody but myself and so, if I scrawl down a few disjointed lines, it is all the information that you will get. But it is more than most people will give you.

Eleven years ago – a pound a week – alone in London. 'So lonely I was,' he told me once, 'I had nobody to speak to but my landlady. And even landladies, after a time, lose their charm. They are the last people who do, but still, it is inevitable.'

'The New Age' – essays for two years – one friend. The friend, oddly enough, was young Frank Henderson, whose delightful old father ties a red tie better than any other Socialist in London, and runs 'The Bomb Shop,' where one may buy the sweetest seditious literature on this side of the English Channel. 'I used to sit at the back of the shop, without a bob, talking to Frank,' he said. 'I still do. We roar with laughter as we see people coming in to buy *Mayfair*.'

The London Venture – £30 profit – a visit to Bruce Ingram, the Editor of *The Sketch* – a commission to do twelve short stories of 1,500 words each, at a remuneration of £8 apiece. 'And now,' he tells me, 'I have a contract for the rest of my life, which brings me in £900 for every short story I write, whether it is published or not. Isn't it silly?'

I liked that remark, 'Isn't it silly?' It is the sort of remark that any young man, with his pockets full of unexpected dollars, might make. He sits down and writes. His stories are sent drifting round the world. They come drifting back. Then, one day, they do not drift back. They are published. They create a sensation. And he is 'made.'

'I have never met anybody who liked my books.' Now that I have put it down, that seems to me the most extraordinary sentence I have ever written. 'Never met anybody who liked my books.' I can see him now, as he said it, propped up against a pile of cushions in his flat in Charles Street. The flat in question is at the extreme end of the street, rather crowded out by its richer relatives, like a raw recruit who has just shuffled hastily into line, and tries to look as though he had been there from the beginning.

'You see,' he went on, 'I'm not really a fashion. I'm a disease. An international disease. Nobody likes me. Most of the people who read me say, "How horrid, or how silly, or how tiresome." And yet they read me. They've *got* to, don't you see? That's really the cleverest thing I did. I saw the rather feverish state of the body politic and social. And I disseminated my poisonous prose right and left. They did not catch it at first. A few people who have been thoroughly inoculated by a habit of taking Wordsworth neat have not caught it even yet. But the great majority have fallen by the wayside. And how they hate it!'

I don't like people who do not adore their mothers. It seems a strange thing to say, just like that, in the middle of this little caper with Michael Arlen, but it is not quite so irrelevant as you think. Michael Arlen is a nice young man, and he adores his mother. The first proceeds of *The Green Hat* may now be seen round Mrs. Arlen's neck, in the shape of a chain of glistening pearls.

'She reads *The Green Hat* serially in an Armenian paper published in Constantinople, which is sent to her in Cheshire,' he told me. 'You see, she hardly speaks a word of English. But,' – and here he looked almost earnest for a moment – 'I defy anybody to tell me that I write English like a foreigner.'

He doesn't. He analysed his style to me as 'influenced by an early study of de Quincy, with a side glance at the eighteenth century.' I think it a very beautiful style. A liqueur style, of course, to be sipped with discretion. But one does not sneer at yellow chartreuse because one cannot turn it on from a tap. There is a lingering cadence about it, a lazy passion, as though he were lying on a sofa by a bowl of roses and picking them to pieces one by one. I shudder at that awful simile. But it shall stand. It vaguely expresses what I mean.

I mentioned yellow chartreuse. Immediately it brought into my mind's eye the huge yellow Rolls-Royce which he suddenly bought, and equally suddenly gave away – (to his mother). Somehow that car seemed to help me to understand him. It was luxurious, and he adores luxury. It was six inches longer than any other car in London, and who would not, in their heart of hearts, delight in that distinction? And it had, on the number plate, M.A. He had taken the car all the way to Manchester to be registered, in order to have that mark put on it. 'It is exactly the sort of car that my sort of success demands,' he said, a little wistfully. It was.

I remember driving round and round Hyde Park in this car, on one of those early summer evenings when one feels one's whole life has been devoted to the consumption of strawberries. We drove round until I felt slightly dizzy. But in spite of the dizziness I remember a great many things we said, for we were in good form just then, and Michael had been lying in bed all day, 'from fatigue.'

'One day,' he said, and his eyes were half closed, 'there will be a house in a square – fountains and silky animals – women. . . .'

I wondered. Silky animals? Women? Which was which? Or was each, neither? If you understand me. . . .

'And,' he said, 'I shall go away, sell everything, go right away.' The car whirled round a corner. 'With two innovation trunks.'

We were on a straight piece of road, and my head was clearer.

'Tell me,' I said, 'about *The Green Hat.*'

'There is nothing to tell.'

There is everything to tell about something which makes one a millionaire.'

'Ah!' The Albert Memorial hove in sight, and we were both silent, and a little awed. Then, 'It was written in two months. At a place called Southport, in Lancashire. I wrote solidly every day for ten hours. Lots of drink and no friends. I would write all the morning. Then, in the afternoon, I would read what I had written. Then in the evening I would re-write it again.'

The Albert Memorial had vanished into the distance, as even Albert Memorials do (which is the consolation of life), and he told me more.

'And on each new morning,' he said, 'I would begin by writing the last two pages over again, to get me into the mood of the thing. There are a hundred thousand words in *The Green Hat*.'

'It makes me feel exceedingly hearty,' I said, 'to think that "we authors"' (you see, the Albert Memorial was still with us in spirit), 'are capable of such a physical strain.'

The car whizzed once more round a bend. 'Look quickly,' I said. 'Over there. A pink chestnut has forgotten the time of year. It ought to have been over long ago. And look at it now. *Please. . . .*' I was becoming agonized.

'I never look at views,' he said, examining his small hands with intense interest.

'A pink chestnut is not a view. It is an emotion.'

He flicked his fingers, and sighed. 'Only people,' he said. 'And streets, of course. But I hate views. Going across America I never looked out of the window. I was too excited by the people inside. Trees and hills and valleys say nothing to me. Weather says very little to me. Environment leaves me cold.'

We had whizzed far enough. I called a halt, and I got out. And Michael Arlen waved his hand with an eighteenth-century grace, the pink chestnut outlining his head like a halo that has missed its way.

Au revoir – you charming person! I seem to see you wandering away from me, rather inconsequently, down one of the grey, misty streets of the Mayfair which you love. You make, in some vague a way, romance even of Berkeley Square. I had always regarded it as dull. But to you, it has a beauty. It tells you so many secrets. And though, in the morning, I feel that I know the answer to those secrets, at night you touch them with magic, you colour them with something of your own subtle spirit.

CHAPTER TWENTY-SIX

Containing the Hideous Truth about Noel Coward

I SHOULD like to draw Noel Coward rather than to talk about him — to take up my pen and trace, with infinite subtlety, the rather bumpy forehead, the keen nose, the darting eyes — the mouth, especially the mouth, which seems constantly on the point of uttering delicious impudences.

But when I draw people, they are always Queen Victoria. They have invariably the same dejected eyelids, the same flaccid lips. Even the addition of a moustache fails to conceal the resemblance. And though Queen Victoria and Noel Coward have much in common — (e.g. an invincible determination, and a well-founded conviction that they are typical of their age) — I must content myself with words, and not with lines.

I first really began to know him one evening before the production of *London Calling*. It was a cold night, there had been a party, and, as far as I remember, a number of us found ourselves in a long, golden room, faintly fragrant with something of Coty's. It was late, but nobody minded, for there was a feeling about the room which was neither of night nor of day, but of that exquisite indetermination which lulls the senses into a lazy oblivion. To complete the picture, you must add an immense couch, covered with green cushions and purple women, and one of those sleek, black pianos that simply demand to be played upon.

It was played upon, by Noel Coward. I wish I could recapture that scene — his curious, agile fingers, the husky voice in which he half sang, half spoke, his lyrics – rather insolently tossing us an occasional spark of wit, drifting with complete indifference, into a line of baroque poetry:

'*Parisian pierrot, society's hero. . . .*'

And all the time, propped up against the piano, a languid French doll was regarding him with painted eyes, as though it were saying, '*You* are the only person who understands me here.'

But it wasn't. I think I understood him, too, rather better than the purple women. For he was outside this curious and typical scene, as a spectator, not as a participator. Even though he was the centre of attraction, he was, in a sense, hovering on the edge of it all, intensely interested, entirely detached. Somebody would say to him, 'Isn't that marvellous?' And though he replied, '*too* marvellous,' with exactly the intonation that was required of him, there was a look in his eyes which suggested that he really meant, 'It is not marvellous at all. And you, my dear, are an empty-headed fool for calling it so.'

'*Parisian pierrot, society's hero. . . .*'

There is more in those four words than most of the amiable young ladies who play it in the wrong key would imagine. Something of a sneer, I believe. I have an imaginary picture in my mind which illustrates the phrase. The party is over, the last cigarette has burnt itself into an obscene mess in the ash tray, the roses have drooped their expensive and artificial heads in a despairing gesture. Only the doll remains alert, staring in front of it with the same painted eyes. This is the doll's hour. And

249

Noel goes up to it, smiling – (I should like to say 'sardonically,' but it sounds too like a tailor's advertisement), and negligently twitches its hand, and fingers its ruff, and probably, as a final gesture of contempt, flicks his finger on its stumpy nose.

As a matter of fact, no such touching scene was enacted after this particular party, for we walked back to my flat together, and there, in an atmosphere devoid of dolls, in front of one of those gas fires which look like skulls roasting in hell, I learnt a great deal about Noel which I had never hitherto suspected.

I learnt, for example, that his first trip to the United States, which was announced with so harmonious a flourish of trumpets, had been accomplished on the sum of £50. 'Nobody would put on any of my plays,' he said. 'There was nothing for me to do in England. So I sold some songs and went to America. I published a book which nobody read. I was a failure. But – oh – how successful I pretended to be.'

That was typical of Noel. His conceit he reserves only for his public. For himself and for his friends he has none at all. That bold and impudent mask with which he covers his real feelings when attacked by the Press is gently lowered as soon as the last reporter has vanished through the front door, and with a sigh he returns to the abnormal, weary of misrepresenting himself to mediocre minds. He is not in the least affected by the numerous women who powder their noses at his newly erected shrine. He demands criticism.

One picture of him will always remain in my mind. It was behind the stage at the Everyman Theatre after the first night of *The Vortex*. Noel was hunched up in a chair in front of a fire, on which a kettle was making pleasant domestic noises. His face was still haggard from the ghastly make-up which he wears in the third Act, and he flaunted a dressing-gown of flowered silk which I have never ceased to covet. We were in semi-darkness. As the firelight flickered, so did our conversation – staccato, a little taut and weary.

'You're terribly kind,' he said. 'And now please tell me the truth.'

'I've told you nothing but the truth.'

'The whole truth?'

I laughed. 'Well – the last Act – the very last few minutes. . . .'

The flowered silk rustled. He was sitting upright. 'Yes?'

'I thought it too indeterminate. You plunged us into that terrible swamp of emotion and you left us there, sticking. I wanted some sort of sign-post. I didn't know whether I was going to sink or swim.'

'I know. You're absolutely right. I muddled that to-night.'

I thought to myself how infuriated I should have been if anybody in that triumphant moment had dared to suggest imperfections, especially if I had asked them to do so.

'There *is* a sign-post,' he went on. 'Just the words, "we'll both try." I meant to say them very clearly. I always shall in future.'

It is the habit among many dreary young men, whose failure in life may be measured by the fault-less fit of their waistcoats, to croon to each other:

'Noel, twenty-five? My dear, he's at least thirty.'
One has the impression that their pockets are
stuffed with the birth certificates of their enemies.
It is not on the tedious evidence of a birth certificate
that I should accept the evidence of Noel's youth.
There have been moments when I have felt, although
we are about the same age, that I was old enough to
be his grandfather.

One such moment was when we were lunching together and he suddenly said, 'I've got a secretary!'
He said it with such gusto, such a ring of glee, that
I felt exactly as though some pink and perfect child
had approached me, saying, 'Look what *I've* got!
And if you wind it up it will run right across to the
fender.' I am sure that Noel's secretary does not
need to be wound up.

On another occasion – (I do trust that I am not
being impertinent. I am only trying to put before
you the real Noel. If he wished to pose as a rich
dilettante whose first epigrams had echoed under
expensive and ancestral roofs, it would be different).
On another occasion, I met him in the street,
strangely enough, opposite a toy shop, and he said,
in an awed whisper, 'I almost bought a manor house
the other day.' There was something magnificent
in that remark. I stood quite still, slightly pale at
the thought, and looked fixedly at one of the most
beautiful golliwogs I have ever seen. 'I almost
bought a manor house.' That wasn't the remark
of a depraved, doped genius. 'I almost bought a
golliwog.' Almost, you note. I knew, and he knew,
in that rare and transient moment, that he could
not really mean what he said. It was only bluff.

It was a doll's house that he was talking about.

That last paragraph is involved, but it is meant to convey to you the spirit for which nobody ever gives him any credit – the spirit of gay adventure which is perhaps the most attractive thing about him.

I wish I could be a Boswell, but I am quite sure that I couldn't. I should always be writing down my own remarks instead of those of other people, which is probably what Boswell really did. And so, out of all the delicious flow of impudences which has sparkled through Noel's lips, I can gather up not one single drop.

But at least one thing I must say – that if Noel Coward could fall in love, he would certainly write a greater play than *The Vortex*, in the truest sense of that much-abused word. It may sound foolish, but I should imagine that he found it exceedingly difficult to fall in love. Love, in the accepted sense of the word, demands quite a great deal of stupidity on the part of both concerned. Most of us have it. Noel hasn't. In the firm contours of his mind there appear none of those unsuspected cracks through which occasionally the divine foolishness may escape. It is as though his brain were like a perfect emerald without a flaw in it, which is a paradox, for as Monsieur Cartier will tell you, no emerald which does not possess a flaw is perfect. One day, I believe, he *will* fall in love, and the prospect is so intriguing that I could close my eyes and allow my pen to scrawl ahead indefinitely at the delicious prospect of Noel singing lyrics ('as clean as a whistle') in the scented darkness outside many magic casements.

And when he does, something amazing is going to

happen. For he writes as a bird flies, swiftly, without looking back. With a bird's-eye view, too, of the theatre, which seems to give to his work a poise and a dexterity which is almost uncanny. He showed me once the original manuscript of *The Vortex*. The words, lightly written in pencil, darted down the pages like a flight of swallows. They were eloquent of the ordered frenzy which produced them.

Finally, when anybody tells me that Noel Coward is 'decadent,' I feel like hitting them across the mouth. Do you realize, you outraged mothers and fathers of England, who sit back in your stalls deploring the depravity of the author of *Fallen Angels*, that you are watching a young man who for sheer pluck can give you all the points in the game? Is it decadent to go on the stage as a little boy, and fight, and fight, and fight, when your own sons are learning to be fools in the numerous academies for English gentlemen which still mysteriously flourish in our midst?

Is it decadent to go on writing, without money, without encouragement, with very few friends, always in the dim hope that one day, perhaps, a play may be produced? And when that play is produced, to see it a commercial failure – and the next play too? And when success comes, at the age of twenty-five, to work harder than ever, to stand up to the critics and to say, 'I don't care a damn'? Is that decadent? Or are you merely being slightly more silly than usual?

CHAPTER TWENTY-SEVEN

In which I allow Myself to be entirely Sentimental.

AND thus, abruptly, I end. A line drawn, a cigarette thrown out of an open window, a pile of manuscript pushed into the corner of one's desk, waiting to be sent to the typist.

And thus, I suppose, youth ends. A line drawn under one's eyes, a sudden realization, as one is laughing or drinking, that the 'stuff which will not endure' has worn itself threadbare. To what purpose? God alone knows. Not I.

I have enjoyed the writing of this book far too much to indulge in any sudden moralizations. But I know my generation, this post-war generation which has so baffled the middle-aged onlookers, who, from the gallery, have watched the dance whirling beneath. And I know that the one thing of which we are always accused – that we live for the moment only – is the one thing of which we are disastrously innocent.

We are none of us living for the moment. We are far too self-conscious for that. We have formulated a creed of which the first principle is that happiness, as an actual emotion, does not exist. 'Happiness,' we proclaim, 'consists either in looking forward to things which will never happen or in remembering things which never have happened.' We are therefore young only as long as we can cheat ourselves, as long as we can go on dressing the future in bright garments, and spinning a web of illusion over the past. But in both cases the kind stuff of imagination has to be produced out of our innermost cells, like spiders forced every day to spin two webs. The process is apt to be exhausting.

And yet – we are constantly forgetting our philosophy. A bright summer morning will do it. An apple tree in fluffy and adorable bloom will do it. Sometimes (for those of us who are most depraved), pink foie gras will do it. But even then, we will not allow that we are happy. We only admit the possibility of happiness – i.e. that there may be some form of heaven, or even a mildly exhilarating hell.

Again – I have done. Twelve o'clock strikes. There should really be slow music playing outside my window, so that I might work myself into a frenzy of pathos at the thought that another day has arrived to carry me on to middle-age. I should rather like to stay, just a little longer. But then – better not. Accept the joke of life for what it is worth. It is not such a very brilliant one, after all. And was there not a man, called Browning, who wrote:

> 'Grow old along with me,
> The best is yet to be.' ?

The End